Table of Contents

DISCUSSION GUIDE • PERSONAL STUDY • REFLECTION SCRIPTURE

OVERVIEW 3

EPISODE 1 - CALLED
MARIANO RIVERA 13

EPISODE 2 - TRANSFORMATION
WILLIE ALFONSO 21

EPISODE 3 - REDEMPTION
KYLE OXFORD 29

EPISODE 4 - RESTORATION
ROBERT AND SHARON IRVING 37

EPISODE 5 - PURPOSE
TOM PATERSON 45

EPISODE 6 - BROTHERHOOD
ACHOS 53

EPISODE 7 - CHOICES
JERRY QUIROZ 61

EPISODE 8 - PAIN
TOMMY GREEN 71

EPISODE 9 - IDENTITY
PROPAGANDA 79

EPISODE 10 - RELOAD
CLINT BRUCE 89

OVERVIEW

WELCOME TO THE CORE SERIES 1 SMALL GROUP EXPERIENCE! WE ARE EXCITED YOU CHOSE TO BE A PART OF THIS JOURNEY.

This is the passion behind CORE: to help men feel alive when they see who they truly are and what they were made for in the context of brotherhood. If you haven't already, check out coreunites.com to keep in touch with other resources and events to help you win the battles over your heart, family and city.

It is important for you to know that the whole reason we have produced the CORE Films and Participant Guide is to help create an environment where you can experience breakthrough in some of the most important areas of your life.

C●RE

In spite of what our culture might tell us, **life was not designed to figure things out on our own.** When Jesus came to earth to start a revolution, he did so by gathering a small band of **ordinary men.**

OVERVIEW

These men had their own unique backgrounds, diverse occupations and individual personalities. It was alongside one another that Jesus would orchestrate learning environments that would change them into the most powerful transformative community in the history of the world.

Together, these men went from being self-centered individuals, to united powerhouses that forever changed the course of history. Jesus didn't just teach them wonderful truths. He modeled, coached and empowered them on what it took to make those truths become a living reality in the challenging world in which they lived. Jesus is still forming and discipling powerful communities today.

Our prayer is that this 10-session small group experience is the beginning of a journey that transforms your group into this type of community.

Here are the basic elements we have prepared for you:

10 SHORT FILMS

We believe in the power of story. The films are stories of real people, facing real life challenges.

10 PART DISCUSSION GUIDE

We believe in the power of community. This guide will help facilitate small group interaction in a way that creates connection around things that matter.

10-PART PERSONAL STUDY & SCRIPTURE READING

We believe in the power of personal study and reflection. This gives the opportunity, between group meetings, to move the ideas from the film and discussion into deeper understanding and growth.

C●RE

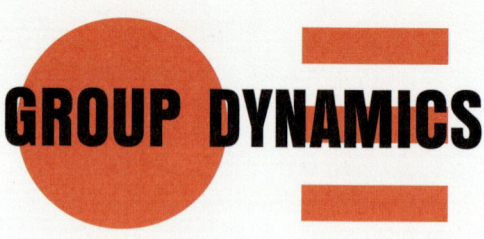

GROUP DYNAMICS

COMBINED WITH THE FILMS, THE 10-SESSION GROUP DISCUSSION IS DESIGNED TO MAXIMIZE INTERACTION, CONNECTION AND MEANINGFUL CONVERSATIONS.

We've intentionally made this guide as straightforward as possible. Please know that each of these simple steps are strategically designed to help create maximum impact for you and those in your group. With that in mind, we encourage you to trust the process by following each step, along with their suggested time frames.

CORE Group time consists of:

1. **Opening Prayer.** Surrendering time and hearts to God's leading.
2. **Check In.** Discussing past week's issues, progress and challenges.
3. **Watch Film.** Viewing together a 10-minute real life story.
4. **Discussion.** Sharing personal impressions and thoughts about the film.
5. **Action.** Establishing measurable steps that can be taken throughout the next week.
6. **Closing Prayer.** Asking for God's guidance and strength for the week ahead.

Each meeting together will serve as an opportunity to connect with each other, get real, build trust and consider the important issues in the lives of everyone in your group.

IDEAL GROUP SIZE & TIME FRAME

An ideal small group size is 5-7. If the group is too small and somebody does not come or drops out, you can lose the collective perspective and encouragement a group can bring. If it is too large, you lose the opportunity for everyone to fully participate and build trust. If your group is larger, you can break into smaller groups for the Discussion and Action time.

An ideal time frame for your group is 90 minutes. Of course, if your group decides, you can meet for longer periods of times. You can also meet for shorter periods. We recommend not meeting for less than 60 minutes. The suggested meeting agenda we have provided is based on the 90-minute time frame. If you meet longer or shorter, adjust accordingly.

OVERVIEW

GROUP LEADER

The most effective small groups have one individual who will organize and guide the meetings. They will help with the communication necessary for meeting times and reminders in between gatherings. If you prefer as a group, you can have multiple group members coordinate a session and rotate between them. If one individual is motivated to "owning" the group logistics and reminders for the full 10-weeks, this will go a long way in seeing the group stay consistent and finish strong.

MEETING LOGISTICS

The group dynamic is designed around watching a short film together each time you meet. This will require having access to a proper screen and sound system. Additionally, Wi-Fi access or a DVD player is crucial. In choosing the meeting place, the fewer distractions you have, the greater the chance for open discussion. Some churches host larger gatherings of men that are sitting around individual tables. They all watch the film together and participate in all the discussion time at their tables. If you do this, to build trust, we encourage you to keep the same guys at each table, each week.

1st SESSION ORIENTATION

Please be sure your group goes over the Sharing and Group Guidelines in the first session and has a chance to ask any clarification questions. Have the group agree to commit to these Guidelines. They are simple yet designed to enhance your experience together.

Here is how everything fits together for this CORE Series 1.

Each meeting you will go through the Group Discussion Guide, watch a film and discuss personal relevance and application.

- In between each session, you will go through the Personal Study and Scripture Reflection to process the major theme of that film and think more deeply on supporting scriptures.

- At the next meeting you will have an opportunity to discuss what you discovered, worked through, and what stood out to you during your Personal Study and Scripture Reflection time.

We highly recommend you schedule one or two times between sessions to enjoy a shared activity together as a group (BBQ, movie, sporting event, weekend getaway, etc.). The purpose of this is to help facilitate getting to know each other in a different kind of environment. Be creative and plan something everyone will enjoy.

CORE

In your opening Episode 1 small group session, please **read out loud these guidelines** for everyone to agree to.

OVERVIEW

PERSONAL SHARING GUIDELINES

1. **Personalize, Not Sermonize.**
   What does the specific consideration being discussed mean for my life, my concerns, my dreams versus giving additional insights to others. Speak more from the "I" and "my" and not "we" and "you." (Can be difficult for those who are teachers or those who wish to be seen as insightful.)

2. **Be Brief.**
   Be thoughtful not to dominate discussion time. Think in terms of 1-2 minutes each time you share. If you have something that needs more time to unpack, make a request to discuss later. (Can be difficult for those who externally process versus those who internalize thoughts before speaking.)

3. **Encourage, Not Fix.**
   We honor courageous authenticity. We discourage group counsel or correction. (Can be difficult for those who are counselors or fixers.)

4. **Maintain Confidentiality.**
   Keep everything shared confidential. Do not repeat it to ANYONE outside your CORE group, including spouses or close friends. (Can be difficult for those who don't highly value being a trusted confidante.)

GROUP GUIDELINES

1. Take responsibility for your own actions, results and experience.
2. Real, honest and transparent discussion is highly encouraged.
3. As mentioned in the Personal Sharing Guidelines, maintain confidentiality.
4. If you are going to be late or absent, call someone in your group to inform them.
5. No cellphone use during the meeting, unless permission is asked at the beginning of the meeting.
6. Don't leave the group permanently without speaking to your group about it.

CORE

There are 10-film episodes in CORE Series 1. So, you have **10 small group meetings and personal reflection opportunities** revolving around each episode.

OVERVIEW

ADDITIONAL GROUP BEST PRACTICES

In these groups, we put a premium on being real. No posing required. "Being real" can mean different things to different people. So, be respectful of each other and embrace what "being real" means for them.

- Interrupt any tendency you feel to judge another.
- Avoid being a "professional advice giver." If someone in the group wants input or feedback, let them ask for it. If you have input you want to offer, ask permission to give it. Feel free to not grant permission to someone to give input if you are not ready to hear it. Be committed to creating an honoring and respectful environment in your group.
- Do not shut down someone who is using strong language or expressing raw emotion in describing their perspective and experience, i.e., swearing, raising voice, etc.
- Be respectful and aware of the time frames included in the group meeting agenda for each week. A common problem for groups is the tendency of one guy to dominate the group time. If someone is going over on time, after the meeting, respectfully remind them of the time so they can limit their sharing time. If they persist, gently remind them during the group time.
- There will be some very good and open conversations in the Check In and Discussion time. The temptation will be to let that take so much of the group time that you sacrifice the Action round. The current spiritual culture is high on talking but slow on doing. When you purposefully give time to ask, "what specific step am I going to take this week?", it can move your group into new levels of discovery and breakthrough. This also gives everyone something specific to pray for one another during the week.
- When you discuss how your previous week's Action step went, this is a "no shame zone" if someone is still struggling. Growth takes time. Empathy, encouragement, and patience will go a long way to building the kind of environment that will surface root issues and facilitate breakthrough.
- The focus of discussion in these CORE group meetings is authentic sharing, encouraging, and connecting. The focus for the Discussion time is not instructing, teaching, or pontificating. Of course, you can offer suggestions, just be aware that this is an opportunity for your group to open up with what they are processing and discovering.
- A great CORE group meeting, which takes time to evolve, has an ease and a flow to it. It is not a rigidly enforced agenda, but it is important to follow the established guidelines that allow enough time for each of the group elements.

LET'S GO!

EPISODE

MARIANO RIVERA
CALLED

GROUP DISCUSSION GUIDE
90 MINUTES

Opening Prayer
Surrender time and heart to God's leading.

Check In
(15 minutes - 1 to 2 minutes each)

1. Share name.
2. Reasons for being in the group.
3. One thing you would like to get from participating in the group.

Together Read the Guidelines on Page 10. (10 minutes)

These are simple yet designed to enhance your group experience.

1. Does everyone in the group understand them?
2. Are there any clarification questions regarding any of the guidelines?
3. Can we commit to these as a group?

Note: Many of you are seeing this Participant Guide for the first time. There is some foundational information in the Overview and Group Dynamics section in this booklet that would be well worth reading before you meet again.

Watch Film (10 minutes)
Mariano Rivera - Called

Discussion (45 minutes)
Be mindful of the need for everyone to have the opportunity to talk. Take 1-2 minutes each time you share.

1. Which part of Mariano's story did you connect with?
2. Mariano said that his pitch's new movement was not something he deserved or was asking for but was a gift that gave him a platform to honor God. Have you ever thought that way about a strength or ability in your life? Explain.

Action (10 minutes)
In light of today's discussion, what is one step you can take in your life or in your relationships this week? Something specific. Something measurable. Something the group can pray for during the week.

Read Out Loud This Special Note
The Personal Study and Scripture Reflection section in this guide is included in each of the sessions. Taking time each week to do them is one of the most important things you choose to do over these next 10 weeks. It is the difference between randomly throwing seed on the ground versus planting it deeply. Setting aside time for personal study and prayerful reflection is a new rhythm for many. Choosing to commit to this, along with showing up every week with your group, will strengthen your ability to drop old thoughts and habits and take on new ways to think and live.

Closing Prayer
Ask for God's guidance and strength for the week ahead.

PERSONAL STUDY

EPISODE 1: MARIANO RIVERA - CALLED

Given Mariano's status as the greatest relief pitcher in the history of baseball, it might at first be hard to relate to how his journey began. It started with him having virtually no awareness of a particular calling or specific purpose. Calling and purpose were probably the furthest things from his mind. Yet, regardless of what Mariano was or was not aware of, it is clear from his story that God had a calling and purpose for his life.

In the same way, God has a specific calling and purpose for you. Look at what He says to you in His word:

You did not choose me, but I chose you and appointed you so that you might go and bear fruit—fruit that will last—and so that whatever you ask in my name the Father will give you. **John 15:16 (NIV)**

God chose the lowly things of this world and the despised things—and the things that are not—to nullify the things that are, so that no one may boast before him. **1 Corinthians 1:28-29 (NIV)**

God has a purpose for His people. It's such a wild thought, isn't it? The God of the universe has chosen to collaborate with ordinary – everyday – imperfect people. He doesn't do this because He's been forced to and it's definitely not because He needs to… but solely because He wants to.

God made you in His image. **Genesis 1:27 (ESV)** clearly states our original purpose and calling:

"So God created man in his own image, in the image of God he created him; male and female he created them."

This means that the all-encompassing aim of your life is to reflect God to others. That looks uniquely different for each one of us. We all have different jobs, different families, live in different homes, have different backgrounds, etc. But, there are some constants for everyone - like reflecting God's love, His goodness, His compassion, His forgiveness, just to name a few. All of us are called to reflect God to others, and we all have specific people, places and times that we get to reflect Him.

When you get a glimpse of the life of Mariano Rivera, you see the uniqueness of God's calling. We're talking about the best closer in major league history. When he stepped on the mound in the ninth inning, he dominated unlike anyone before or after him. But his story is much more than being a great pitcher. It's a love story of God pursuing him, changing him and collaborating with him.

GOD MADE MARIANO IN HIS OWN IMAGE, AND GOD LED HIM TO A PARTICULAR PLACE, WITH A PARTICULAR TALENT, TO SHOW GOD'S CHARACTER TO A PARTICULAR PEOPLE.

Even before Mariano committed his life to Christ, he became aware that God was trying to get his and his wife's attention. God had been using each of Mariano's circumstances to soften his heart and to open his eyes. One day, he heard a pastor give an invitation to become a follower of Jesus. It was then, on

THE TWO MOST IMPORTANT DAYS IN YOUR LIFE ARE THE DAY YOU WERE BORN AND THE DAY YOU FOUND OUT WHY.

Mark Twain

EPISODE 1

that day, that he confessed Jesus as his Lord and made Him his Savior.

If you openly declare that Jesus is Lord and believe in your heart that God raised him from the dead, you will be saved. For it is by believing in your heart that you are made right with God, and it is by openly declaring your faith that you are saved. **Romans 10:9-10 (NLT)**

Mariano said, "That was the moment that I said, 'I surrender. I can't do this thing anymore.' That moment was something special... I said to God, whatever you want us to do, we are here."

He began to see with more and more clarity, that God was weaving His grand story within the particulars of his own human story.

Mariano started noticing God's work in very specific things, including baseball. For example, when Mariano threw the ball – just as he always had – it started moving toward the catcher in ways that he had never experienced before. Batters were rarely able to get a hit off his pitches, and Mariano knew that God had given him this particular ability for a purpose.

Mariano said, "It was something that the Lord gave me to give me a platform to talk about Him. Not because I was asking. Not because I deserved it. But He wanted to use that to glorify his name."

This is indeed a gift - God giving something that was not earned or expected. A gift is not based upon accomplishments, dedication, hard work, talent or effort. <u>A gift is something that the Giver has decided to impart simply because He wants to and loves to.</u>

How many gifts from God go unnoticed or unappreciated for what they are? It is so easy to experience blessings in our relationships and careers without seeing them for what they really are. They are all opportunities to experience the graciousness of God in our lives and to use them to honor Him.

<u>We use the gifts that God has given us in one of two ways</u>: <u>to honor God, or to honor ourselves</u>. Oftentimes we can start believing that we are the ones who are responsible for these gifts in our lives. But Mariano shares with us that it's through the difficult times of life that we are reminded of how powerless we really are - and how powerful God is. It is when things don't turn out the way we want them, when we go through times of failure and unmet expectations, that we are given the gift of facing our own inabilities.

<u>Here is a secret worth discovering</u>: <u>when we come face to face with inabilities and weaknesses and learn how to surrender those to the King of Grace,</u> t<u>here exists freedom and joy</u>. It is as simple as praying, "God I can't do this, I can't face this, but I ask you to help me take the first steps to let you do through me what I'm struggling with on my own."

This is what Paul is encouraging the Corinthians with the counterintuitive secret God revealed to him.

But he said to me, My grace is sufficient for you, for my power is made perfect in weakness. Therefore I will boast all the more gladly of my weaknesses, so that the power of Christ may rest upon me.
2 Corinthians 12:9 (NIV)

MARIANO RIVERA - CALLED

Are you willing to see hardships that way? Ask yourself this CRUCIAL question:

▶ When I go through the fire of life's challenges, am I willing to become less dependent on myself and more dependent on God?

We must believe that we can face our own weakness because God is always seeking to draw our hearts closer to Him — and few things in the world can draw us nearer to God than difficulties. He is always faithful to grant us the grace and courage necessary to stand firm during these times. When we come out of that fire, we will be stronger and more faithful than when we went into it.

<u>One of the ways we are able to persevere with hope is by the gift of community</u>. Mariano said that Willie Alfonso was a powerful influence during the hardest seasons of his life. Willie was a person who was always there for Mariano. He was one of God's provisions for Mariano to recognize that life is not meant to be figured out on his own.

As you think about those in your CORE group:

- Trust that God has provided them for you to encourage and strengthen your faith.
- Trust that God has provided you for them to encourage and strengthen their faith.

God has gathered each of you together to be a support for one another through the fires.

Think about the challenges you currently face in your life - work, family, children, spouse, and all the other facets of your life. Let this ten-week CORE journey be an opportunity to be as real as possible with one another, to come alongside one another and to experience significant breakthroughs together.

SESSION 1
REFLECTION

PERSONAL STUDY QUESTIONS

1. In what area of my life could I really use a breakthrough?
2. What fears do I have that could create obstacles to seeing God work in and through me?
3. Have I addressed my Action step that I shared with my CORE Group? If not, what is keeping me from stepping out and addressing it? What's my next step?

JOURNALING:

Write down your answers to the three personal study questions above in a notebook. Then, each week, as you watch a new film and the themes contained within it, write down what comes to mind that can be applied to the specific areas in your life where you are committed to taking new ground.

Write down every week what you are learning. This can include: what is happening, what you're experiencing, where you are making progress, where you are stuck, what's working, what's not working, what's wanted and needed, what's next.

A quick encouragement to writing these answers down:
It may not seem very important right now, but it will be incredibly beneficial to take the time to write down your answers to the questions each week. Start your own simple notebook. There are things that come to mind and become clearer when you pause to write. "Thinking" and/or "talking" alone don't produce the same kind of meaningful insight as writing. These are powerful little moments that give you opportunities to go below the surface of typical and familiar thoughts and face blind spots and discover new ways to replace lies with truth.

Note: Your notebook is also a great place to write down the Action steps and prayer requests for you and your group. You can use this as a reminder on what you are wanting to take new ground in and to pray for the guys in your group during the week.

SCRIPTURE REFLECTION:

We encourage you to consider the following scripture passage over the course of this week in a contemplative way. Read the passage four separate times. It works well if you read it on four separate days. But, each time you read it, you read it from a different perspective.

1. With the first reading, be alert for a phrase or word that stands out for you.

2. During the second reading, take a moment to reflect on what touches you—perhaps saying that particular verse out loud or writing it in your notebook.

3. After reading the passage a third time, respond with a prayer to God about what you have experienced and what the scripture might be calling you to.

4. Finally, rest in silence after a fourth reading, trusting that, *"it is God who works in you, both to will and to work for his good pleasure."* **Philippians 2:13 (ESV)**

This process helps you to engage not only your mind, but also your heart and soul in worshipful reflection on the scriptures.

This week's reflection scripture: **EPHESIANS 2:4-10 (NIV)**

But God, being rich in mercy, because of the great love with which he loved us, even when we were dead in our trespasses, made us alive together with Christ—by grace you have been saved— and raised us up with him and seated us with him in the heavenly places in Christ Jesus, so that in the coming ages he might show the immeasurable riches of his grace in kindness toward us in Christ Jesus.

For by grace you have been saved through faith. And this is not your own doing; it is the gift of God, not a result of works, so that no one may boast. For we are his workmanship, created in Christ Jesus for good works, which God prepared beforehand, that we should walk in them.

EPISODE

WILLIE ALFONSO
TRANSFORMATION

GROUP DISCUSSION GUIDE
90 MINUTES

Opening Prayer
Surrender time and heart to God's leading.

Check In (25 minutes)
Be mindful of the need for everyone to have the opportunity to talk. Take 1-2 minutes each time you share.

1. How has your week gone? Family? Work?

2. What kind of progress or challenges did you have with your Action step?

3. How was your Personal Study and Scripture Reflection time this week? What is resonating? What is not working?

Check In time is high on encouragement and low on "judgment".

Watch Film (10 minutes)
Willie Alfonso - Transformation

Discussion (45 minutes)
1. Which part of Willie's story did you connect with?

2. Briefly share what was positive and negative about the relationship with your father/step-father. How do you think that relationship impacted your life and decisions?

Action (10 minutes)
Be mindful of the need for everyone to have an opportunity to talk. Take 2-3 minutes each. Take notes and pray for each other's Action steps during the week. As always, keep everything confidential.

In light of today's discussion, what is one step you can take in your life or in your relationships this week? Something specific. Something measurable. Something the group can pray for during the week.

Closing Prayer
Ask for God's guidance and strength during the week ahead.

WHAT LIES BEHIND US AND WHAT LIES BEFORE US ARE TINY MATTERS COMPARED TO WHAT LIES WITHIN US.

Ralph Waldo Emerson

PERSONAL STUDY

EPISODE 2: WILLIE ALFONSO - TRANSFORMATION

One of the great themes of last week's Mariano Rivera story is that God calls you and gives gifts to you in order to fulfill that calling. He has made you in His image. He chose you. He loves you. And you did absolutely nothing to earn it. That is the good news of God's grace! No pressure to earn it, perform for it, or try to achieve it. God freely offers it. He paid the price in full. It is a free gift (Romans 5:15; 6:23).

Consider the status of Mariano's life when God called him. It was well before Mariano had accomplished any level of success in his life. God did not choose him because he was successful - because at that time he wasn't. God chose him because God loved him, and it was for God's purposes. God is on the move and He's chosen to use ordinary people to partner with Him and His purposes. Like He invited Mariano to collaborate with Him, He is inviting us to do the same.

Willie Alfonso is the mutual friend that has stood by Mariano for many, many years. They've committed to meet regularly, to be real with each other, and to pursue their love for God together. Their friendship reflects what is at the core of life as brothers. In the same way, this is what's possible for you and those in your group.

Just as Mariano has his unique story, Willie's own story shows the power of God's redemptive grace. To see what Willie's upbringing was like, it's nothing short of the power of God that he is who he is now – and where he is now. Today, Willie serves as the chaplain of the New York Yankees and is involved in serving God and others in a myriad of ways. But that's not how his story began.

Growing up, Willie endured tremendous suffering and rejection:

- He was abused by his violent father.
- He was abandoned by his father and mother.
- He was homeless, sleeping and eating on the streets of New York at 11-years old.
- He experienced deep rejection.
- He was a drug addict.
- He felt deep anger and bitterness towards his father.

And, yet, God rescued him from all of that.

Perhaps your background is not as dramatic as Willie's. Perhaps it's even worse. Regardless, we all experience loss, betrayal, and failure in some form or another. A harmful tendency we have in response to these hardships is to excuse, minimize or dismiss them as not relevant or not a big deal. But they have influenced us just the same.

Willie recounted the persistence of a co-worker that shared an alternative to the self-destructive path he was on. This man told Willie that there was forgiveness found in Jesus. Willie received the gift of God's grace and began learning how to live as an empowered follower of Jesus.

Oftentimes we hear about a person's radical life-change, and it sounds almost too good to be true. We might even become envious of such a powerful story, because we have a hard time seeing our own lives being changed that way. It is easy to assume that a person's outward transformation is more glamorous and immediate than it really is.

EPISODE 2

How does a life like Willie's change so radically? How did Willie get his life turned around?

Though there were many contributing factors, Willie says that it was the daily influence of God's Word that shaped this profound life-change. The Scriptures showed him a new way of addressing the challenges of his life and softened his heart so that he could see those challenges differently.

Here's what Willie says about this:

"I love the Word of God. I think there's an eighteen-inch difference between what you believe here (in your head), and what you transfer here, to your heart. I read the Word of God just about every day."

"You know Psalms 119 says, thy word I have hidden in your heart so that I might not sin against God. I can't tell you how many times I read my Bible in the morning, went outside and that day I ran into a struggle and that verse I read bailed me out."

"I had a guy cut me off not too long ago. I chased this dude down to the red light. I can't tell you what I was thinking. I wasn't chasing him to get him saved! And when I caught up to him I told him, 'Roll your window down, my man.' Then I love how the truth of God comes. The Bible says at the moment of temptation God will always give you the way of escape. You know what God said? 'Yo stupid! What are you doing man? You're about to bang this thing up.'"

"I make it my business to stay in the Word of God, and I also make it my business to hear God speak to me and respond right then."

"My father may have never told me he loved me, but my Heavenly Father tells me every single day. 'Willie, you're special. I love you. I have something special for you to do that only you can do'."

Willie shared one of the most important keys in experiencing a breakthrough in how you are living. He doesn't see reading scripture as something he is supposed to do as a "good" Christian. He sees it in the same way a soldier would view his weapon. It gives him what he needs to face the challenges ahead.

A starting point is reading, reflecting and declaring the truth of what God says is true about who we are. We are sons of the Creator of the Universe. This understanding is the starting point of replacing old self-destructive habits with new ways of thinking and living.

Willie admits that this process is not finished and that he is continually being changed. But it's important that we have a clear view of how he is changing. It wasn't like he just prayed a prayer or snapped his fingers, and then became a changed man. Instead, just as Willie shared, it was how God's Word not only enabled him to see the ways he needed to change but gave him the strength and wisdom to carry out his divine purpose to make a difference in others.

- He embraced God's truth in scripture and studied it.
- He reflected upon it.
- He applied it in his life.
- He allowed it to instruct, challenge and encourage him.

- He applied discipline to this process. He became a disciple—a disciplined one.
- He embraced the possibility of being transformed by the renewing of his mind.
- He made his Action step to hear and obey.

Learning, examining and applying the truth of God from His Word is inwardly life-giving, and outwardly life-changing.

For the word of God is living and active, sharper than any two-edged sword, piercing to the division of soul and of spirit, of joints and of marrow, and discerning the thoughts and intentions of the heart. **Hebrews 4:12 (ESV)**

Willie poured himself into studying and reflecting on scripture. In doing so, he was replacing the lies of the corrupt culture that brought him up, with the life-giving truth of God.

In obeying the Word of God:

- Willie replaced bitterness and rejection with forgiveness and acceptance.
- He replaced isolation with connected brotherhood.
- He replaced abandonment with community.
- He replaced using drugs with being freed by God and being used for His perfect purposes.
- He replaced self-centered survival with other-centered service.

All of us have a past that has shaped us. For better or worse – we all have people and circumstances that have shaped how we see God, how we see ourselves and how we see others. Our history, personality and experiences have a way of convincing us of what is true – even when it's not. Graciously, God has given us His Word so that we can confidently know how to think, how to see and how to live.

EPISODE 2
REFLECTION

PERSONAL STUDY QUESTIONS

1. How did your relationship with your father influence how you are living out your life today?
2. Where do you need to exercise forgiveness for others in order to more fully experience freedom and God's forgiveness for you?
3. Have I addressed my Action step that I shared with my CORE Group? If not, what is keeping me from stepping out and addressing it? What's my next step?

JOURNALING:

Write your answers in your notebook. Also, journal about what comes to mind that can be applied to the specific areas in your life you are committed to taking new ground, as referenced in your vision you created in Session 1. What are you learning? What is happening? Where are you making progress? Where are you stuck? What's working? What's not working? What's wanted and needed? What's next?

SCRIPTURE REFLECTION:

We encourage you to consider this following scripture passage over the course of this week in a contemplative way. Read the passage four separate times. It works well if you read it on four separate days. Each time you read it, read it from a different perspective.

1. With the first reading, be alert for a phrase or word that stands out for you.

2. During the second reading, take a moment to reflect on what touches you, perhaps saying that particular verse out loud or writing it in your notebook.

3. After reading the passage a third time, respond with a prayer to God about what you have experienced and what the scripture might be calling you to.

4. Finally, rest in silence after a fourth reading, trusting that, *"it is God who works in you, both to will and to work for his good pleasure."* **Philippians 2:13 (ESV)**

This process helps you to engage not only your mind, but your heart and soul in worshipful reflection on the scriptures. This can also give you fresh courage and trust to take new ground to where God is calling you forward.

Here is this week's reflection scripture: **PSALM 119:9-16 (ESV)**

How can a young man keep his way pure? By guarding it according to your word. With my whole heart I seek you; let me not wander from your commandments! I have stored up your word in my heart, that I might not sin against you. Blessed are you, O Lord; teach me your statutes! With my lips I declare all the rules of your mouth. In the way of your testimonies I delight as much as in all riches. I will meditate on your precepts and fix my eyes on your ways. I will delight in your statutes; I will not forget your word.

EPISODE

KYLE OXFORD REDEMPTION

GROUP DISCUSSION GUIDE
90 MINUTES

Opening Prayer
Surrender time and heart to God's leading.

Check In (25 minutes)
1. How has your week gone? Family? Work?
2. What kind of progress or challenges did you have with your Action step?
3. How was your Personal Study and Scripture Reflection time this week? What is resonating? What is not working?

Watch Film (10 minutes)
Kyle Oxford - Redemption

Discussion (45 minutes)
1. Which part of Kyle's story did you connect with?
2. Where have you seen God redeem losses in your life or those around you? Explain.

Action (10 minutes)
Be mindful of the need for everyone to have an opportunity to talk. Take 2-3 minutes each. Take notes and pray for each other's action steps during the week. As always, keep everything confidential.

In light of today's discussion, what is one step you can take in your life or in your relationships this week? Something specific. Something measurable. Something the group can pray for during the week.

Closing Prayer
Ask for God's guidance and strength during the week ahead.

PERSONAL STUDY

EPISODE 3: KYLE OXFORD - REDEMPTION

Knowing that you're made in the image of God and that God invites you to reflect Him to others is a captivating thought. It puts wind in your sails like nothing or nobody else could.

There is a calling, but there is also an assault.

The Scriptures remind us that there are forces that actively seek to keep us from experiencing our intended design and purpose. It's often difficult for many to understand, but there is a spiritual adversary who tries to rob you of hope, faithfulness, and obedience.

1 Peter 5:8 (ESV) tells us to *"Be sober-minded; be watchful. Your adversary the devil prowls around like a roaring lion, seeking someone to devour."*

The reality of this assault is evident in Kyle's story. His dream of marriage and family turned into a nightmare of rejection and emasculation. Kyle's openness allows us to see how the enemy can use people and circumstances to wound us.

But even in the face of hurt, pain and disappointment, God's faithfulness is evident in the way He redeems even the darkest seasons of life.

We all have dark seasons of life, don't we? Maybe you can remember the heaviness of deep sorrow or helplessness. Maybe you have found yourself in that season right now.

In the same way that each of our specific callings look uniquely different, the attacks each of us experience from the enemy look uniquely different.

For some, it's the experience of sudden, life-altering moments that cause deep wounds. For others, the attack is slow and rigorous — spread out over a much longer period of time.

In the boxing ring, sometimes a fighter is knocked out by a quick and powerful blow to the head. Often times, it's the round after round of blows to the body that weakens and drops the defenses. Ultimately, this constant attack is what sets up the blow that ends it.

Whether we want to admit it or not, we are in a war, a war over the domain of our affections and decisions. The question is not whether we are in a war but are we at war? A critical question to consider is how are you going to face and win the battles ahead?

God tells us in **Romans 8:28 (NASB)** that He *"causes all things to work together for good to those who love God, to those who are called according to His purpose."* But when you're in the middle of these grueling and despairing seasons, it often doesn't feel that way. It can feel like the solutions are far away, if they exist at all.

Kyle's story is a striking reminder of how God redeems losses, even when those losses are life altering and life defining.

Here is Kyle's story in his own words, again. As you read through what happened with him, consider the reflective questions in bold fonts. Take out your notebook and write what comes to mind as you consider the reflective questions.

"When I was younger I had dreams… like dreams of being a father and being a husband and being a good husband. When our marriage dissolved it forced me to forget about those dreams. And that began the downward spiral for me."

What expectations and/or dreams have you had that were shattered?

THE MEANING OF REDEMPTION IS THAT WE DO NOT HAVE TO BE OUR HISTORY.

Flannery O'Connor

"After that I was in a season of wandering. I remember just feeling like God didn't care about me or my circumstances. I was in a period of rejecting Him. I remember one day just making my mind up that I didn't care what He thought. I didn't care if He existed. I was going to do my own thing because surely it wouldn't or couldn't hurt any more than I already hurt."

Have you ever rebelled against God because of being hurt or disappointed?

"I had the first real conversation that I ever had with God that morning. I said I don't know who you are, I believe that you're there, but I need you to help me, and rescue me out of this. I just laid down on the trail and cried out to God. I wasn't asking for a favor. I wasn't asking for my life to be blessed. I wasn't asking for anything really but for him to have mercy on me."

Kyle cried out to God. He held nothing back and was as real with God as he knew how to be. Where in your life do you need to get entirely real with God and have this kind of conversation?

"Just facing myself and facing God and saying, "I need you" was tough. I felt so unworthy of anything...even a response. But He was faithful and showed up and He met me where I was."

God responds when we are brutally honest and vulnerable with Him. David's example in the Psalms of raw authenticity is a great example of this.

"After I had cried out to God and was reconciled to him, some of the dreams I'd had as a kid started coming back to me and the dreams that I had on my wedding day years before were coming back. I realized that I needed to start moving in the direction of the dreams that God had put before me. And Megan is somebody that was my ideal. She was number one in terms of the kind of woman that I wanted to be with."

What does it tell you about God's character that he loves to surprise us with gifts that are undeserved?

"I don't believe that God's plan was for me to get divorced or for Megan's husband to die and leave behind a widow with two kids. But I do believe that God is really good at taking the broken pieces and making something beautiful out of them. The life that I have now is beyond what I had ever imagined or dreamed of and I'm really excited about the future that I have with Megan and with our kids. I'm excited to see what God does next."

Have you ever experienced a time where God took something broken and turned it into something beautiful?

All of our stories look different on the outside, but at their core they are truly the same. We have our own circumstances, our own day to day realities, but just like everyone, we know the feeling of struggle.

John 10:10 (NKJV) *The thief does not come except to steal, and to kill, and to destroy. I have come that they may have life, and that they may have it more abundantly.*

You have an adversary. Along the course of your life, you're going to take some big hits. But, God is more powerful, and He redeems losses. You can trust Him, and you can turn to Him even in the darkest of seasons. Why? Because Jesus understands and paid the ultimate price to allow you bold access to God's mercy and grace.

This High Priest of ours understands our weaknesses, for he faced all of the same testings we do, yet he did not sin. So let us come boldly to the throne of our gracious God. There we will receive his mercy, and we will find grace to help us when we need it most.
Hebrews 4:15-16 (NLT)

EPISODE 3
REDEMPTION

PERSONAL STUDY QUESTIONS

1. What dreams have you given up on that you desire God to restore?

2. Is there an area of "brokenness" in your life that you could wait expectantly for God to redeem into something beautiful?

3. Have I addressed my Action step that I shared with my CORE Group? If not, what is keeping me from stepping out and addressing it? What's my next step?

JOURNALING:

Write your answers in your notebook. Also, journal about what comes to mind that can be applied to the specific areas in your life you are committed to taking new ground, as referenced in your vision you created in session 1. What are you learning, what is happening, where are you making progress, where are you stuck, what's working, what's not working, what's wanted and needed, what's next?

SCRIPTURE REFLECTION:

We encourage you to consider this following scripture passage over the course of this week in a contemplative way. Read the passage four separate times. It works well if you read it on four separate days. Each time you read it, read it from a different perspective.

1. With the first reading, be alert for a phrase or word that stands out for you.
2. During the second reading, take a moment to reflect on what touches you, perhaps saying that particular verse out loud or writing it in your notebook.
3. After reading the passage a third time, respond with a prayer to God about what you have experienced and what the scripture might be calling you to.
4. Finally, rest in silence after a fourth reading, trusting that, *"it is God who works in you, both to will and to work for his good pleasure."* **Philippians 2:13 (ESV)**

This process helps you to engage not only your mind, but your heart and soul in worshipful reflection on the scriptures. This can also give you fresh courage and trust to take new ground in what God is calling you into next.

This week's reflection scripture: **1 PETER 5:6-11 (NIV)**

Humble yourselves, therefore, under the mighty hand of God so that at the proper time he may exalt you, casting all your anxieties on him, because he cares for you.

Be sober-minded; be watchful. Your adversary the devil prowls around like a roaring lion, seeking someone to devour. Resist him, firm in your faith, knowing that the same kinds of suffering are being experienced by your brotherhood throughout the world.

And after you have suffered a little while, the God of all grace, who has called you to his eternal glory in Christ, will himself restore, confirm, strengthen, and establish you. To him be the dominion forever and ever. Amen.

EPISODE

THE IRVINGS RESTORATION

GROUP DISCUSSION GUIDE
90 MINUTES

Opening Prayer
Surrender time and heart to God's leading.

Check In (25 minutes)
Be mindful of the need for everyone to have opportunity to talk. Take 1-2 minutes each time you share.

1. How has your week gone? Family? Work?
2. What kind of progress or challenges did you have with your Action step?
3. How was your Personal Study and Scripture Reflection time this week? What is resonating? What is not working?

Check In time is high on encouragement and low on "accountability".

Watch Film (10 minutes)
Sharon and Robert Irving - Restoration

Discussion (45 minutes)
This is an opportunity to share from a personal perspective. How is this impacting me? Not a time to share general insights.

1. Which part of Sharon and Robert's story did you connect with?
2. What relationships do you have that might need to be reconciled? What do you desire for those relationships?

Action (10 minutes)
Be mindful of the need for everyone to have an opportunity to talk. Take 2-3 minutes each. Take notes and pray for each other's action steps during the week. As always, keep everything confidential.

In light of today's discussion, what is one step you can take in your life or in your relationships this week? Something specific. Something measurable. Something the group can pray for during the week.

Closing Prayer
Ask for God's guidance and strength during the week ahead.

PERSONAL STUDY

EPISODE 4: ROBERT & SHARON IRVING – RESTORATION

The Irvings are in the midst of a real life, real time reconciliation. In their story, the transparency displayed between them as they struggled to resolve their disappointments into deeper love and connection is inspiring.

Often, when the nature of a relationship is breaking down or is not what we desire, we tend to think, it is what it is. It doesn't occur to us that there is a possibility of restarting the relationship into something deeper, more connected and more fulfilling. It may seem like the current state of the relationship is out of your hands, and that helpless feeling often continues into adulthood.

But, guess what? God says we are given the *ministry of reconciliation*. First, there needs to be personal reconciliation between our Heavenly Father and us, which in turn, will naturally stir up seeking out reconciliation with others. He is the God who sent His Son to reconcile us back into relationship with Him. We get to reflect Him to others by being Ambassadors – Ambassadors of The Reconciler. **(2 Corinthians 5:18-20)**

This applies most powerfully in reconciling lost relationships. To reconcile means to bring back together that which has been separated. Where better to start than in the key relationships of your life that are estranged?

An appropriate place to start is by giving some thought about each of your relationships. What is the status of your rapport with your mom or dad, your step-parents, your children, your spouse, your ex-spouse, co-worker, boss, friends, or acquaintances? In those relationships, where do you regret dropping the ball, or making a mess of things?

Robert Irving's commitment to his work and travel schedule had a significant impact on his family. Tragically, this is not an isolated story – it's a very common one. It happens all the time as our commitment to work and success can become a counterfeit god. We can find ourselves willing to be mediocre in the most important things, to pursue excellence in lesser things. We might start embracing this with good intentions (paying the bills, supporting the family, etc.) without having a clear awareness of the impact it's having on those we love.

What you have to offer others is far more valuable than a paycheck or material provision. Though we must do everything possible to provide for our families, our greatest contributions are in the things that aren't immediately visible. Let's be honest; meeting the demanding challenges of work can feel far more satisfying than the relational challenges a husband and father face.

When you go to the beach and start swimming in ocean waters, many times you'll notice something peculiar. After 5 or 10 minutes of dodging the waves, you'll drift without even being aware. When you look back at where your friends and family are sitting on the beach, you'll notice that the currents have carried you hundreds of feet from where you started. It's typically a very slow and subtle drift.

FORGIVENESS FLOUNDERS BECAUSE I EXCLUDE THE ENEMY FROM THE COMMUNITY OF HUMANS EVEN AS I EXCLUDE MYSELF FROM THE COMMUNITY OF SINNERS.

Miroslav Volf

EPISODE 4

In relationships, our intentions may not be to purposefully neglect what and whom we value the most. Our lack of relational and emotional investment is a series of justifiable circumstances that turn into a subtle, but lifelong drift - a drift that carries us away from what matters most.

As you consider these relationships, keep this in mind: You might notice even the slightest of fractures that need to be addressed and reconciled.

Robert Irving started to address the hurt caused by his absence while Sharon was growing up. Here is what Sharon said about her father's attempts to reconcile more deeply with her.

"To hear him be vulnerable and see him be vulnerable gave me such a different level of respect for him. It definitely did something to my heart, seeing him open up about very hard, uncomfortable things. It was something that, I think I needed, to get to this next level. And for the next chapter of our relationship, it was like a page turned almost."

The Scriptures speak vividly about the priority and impact of reconciliation. While considering your own relationships, let these passages challenge and encourage you.

Matthew 5:23-24 (NIV) *Therefore, if you are offering your gift at the altar and there remember that your brother or sister has something against you, leave your gift there in front of the altar. First go and be reconciled to them; then come and offer your gift.*

Matthew 18:15-16 (ESV) *"If your brother sins against you, go and tell him his fault, between you and him alone. If he listens to you, you have gained your brother."*

The Bible describes the healthiest of relationships as 'iron sharpening iron'. It's a way of consistently seeking out reconciliation with one another. It requires courage, humility and forgiveness. It requires that you be ok with being seen as weak and not being right all the time. It means that you actively seek to work through the breakdown that has occurred with the other. It also requires being vulnerable enough to state what your offense is, if you feel wronged by another. And you not only state it, you then engage a conversation about how to reconcile through it.

Reconciliation creates an avenue for working through the baggage of broken relationships and being at peace with one another. If you don't resolve to work towards reconciliation, the baggage of the brokenness will bleed out on others that you say you care about. Pastor Tim Keller challenges us to take the initiative. "In its most basic and simple form, this teaching is that Christians in community are to never give up on one another, never give up on a relationship, and never write off another believer. We must never tire of forgiving and repenting and seeking to repair our relationships with one another. In short, if any relationship has cooled off or has weakened in any way, it is always your move. It doesn't matter 'who started it:' God always holds you responsible to reach out to repair a tattered relationship. A Christian is responsible to begin the process of reconciliation, regardless of how the distance or the alienation began."

THE IRVINGS - RESTORATION

Jesus' invitation is to not live in resignation, but rather do the work of reconciliation out of a hope for healing and connection. There are no guarantees that it will end in the results you want, but it will always be an opening to soften your heart towards the other, and to lean deeper into empathy, love and compassion for them as you engage in this process.

Our God is a God of love and reconciliation. He calls us to follow his example with one another.

2 Corinthians 5:19, 21 (NLT) *For God was in Christ, reconciling the world to himself, no longer counting people's sins against them. And he gave us this wonderful message of reconciliation. For God made Christ, who never sinned, to be the offering for our sin, so that we could be made right with God through Christ.*

It is never too late to pursue reconciliation when you have been hurt or the one who created the hurt. To do so invites you into the very work of Christ. This has the potential to rewrite your future and transform your legacy.

EPISODE 4
REFLECTION

PERSONAL STUDY QUESTIONS

1. What relationship(s) do you currently have that are in need of reconciliation? What can you do to move towards that possibility?

2. Do you have a parent you desire a more open, connected relationship with? Or perhaps a child? What first steps can you take towards reconciling that relationship? This can be done with parents even after they have passed away. In that case, you work on your relationship towards them in your heart and mind.

3. Take notice of where you hold unforgiveness. Are you willing to start doing the sacred work of forgiving? Can you release them from the desire that they pay for the pain they caused you? This is deeply challenging for some of us. It does cost you something. Draw courage from the truth that your forgiveness cost Jesus everything.

4. Have I addressed my Action step that I shared with my CORE Group? If not, what is keeping me from stepping out and addressing it? What's my next step?

JOURNALING:

Write your answers in your notebook. Also, journal about what comes to mind that can be applied to the specific areas in your life you are committed to in taking new ground, as referenced in your vision you created in Session 1.

— OUR LACK OF RELATIONAL & EMOTIONAL INVESTMENT IS A SERIES OF JUSTIFIABLE CIRCUMSTANCES THAT TURN INTO A SUBTLE, BUT LIFELONG DRIFT — A DRIFT THAT CARRIES US AWAY FROM WHAT MATTERS MOST.

SCRIPTURE REFLECTION:

We encourage you to consider this following scripture passage over the course of this week in a contemplative way. Read the passage four separate times. It works well if you read it on four separate days. Each time you read it, read it from a different perspective.

1. With the first reading, be alert for a phrase or word that stands out for you.

2. During the second reading, take a moment to reflect on what touches you, perhaps saying that particular verse out loud or writing it in your notebook.

3. After reading the passage a third time, respond with a prayer to God about what you have experienced and what the scripture might be calling you to.

4. Finally, rest in silence after a fourth reading, trusting that, *"it is God who works in you, both to will and to work for his good pleasure."* **Philippians 2:13 (ESV)**

This process helps you to engage not only your mind, but your heart and soul in worshipful reflection on the scriptures. This can also give you fresh courage and trust to take new ground to where God is calling you forward.

This week's reflection scripture: **COLOSSIANS 3:12-16 (ESV)**

Put on then, as God's chosen ones, holy and beloved, compassionate hearts, kindness, humility, meekness, and patience, bearing with one another and, if one has a complaint against another, forgiving each other; as the Lord has forgiven you, so you also must forgive.

And above all these put on love, which binds everything together in perfect harmony. And let the peace of Christ rule in your hearts, to which indeed you were called in one body. And be thankful.

Let the word of Christ dwell in you richly, teaching and admonishing one another in all wisdom, singing psalms and hymns and spiritual songs, with thankfulness in your hearts to God.

NIEL — PROPOSAL TO WRITE, STALLING FOR SOME REASON

TODD — INTENTIONALITY W/ WORK & VISITOR FROM INDIANA THAT WILL LEAD TO SOME CHALLENGING MEETINGS. SON'S (29) GIRLFRIEND VISITING, YOUNGEST SON'S DISEASE

EPISODE

5

TOM PATERSON
PURPOSE

GROUP DISCUSSION GUIDE
90 MINUTES

Opening Prayer
Surrender time and heart to God's leading.

Check In (25 minutes)
1. How has your week gone? Family? Work?
2. What kind of progress or challenges did you have with your Action step?
3. How was your Personal Study and Scripture Reflection time this week? What is resonating? What is not working?

Watch Film (10 minutes)
Tom Paterson - Purpose

Discussion (45 minutes)
1. Which part of Tom's story or what Pete (the narrator for this film) shared connected with you?
2. What are you clear about regarding your purpose?
3. Pete said once we are settled in knowing our identity as God's son, we can be free to live out our divine purpose. How do you think that idea would impact you and your purpose?

Action (10 minutes)
Be mindful of the need for everyone to have an opportunity to talk. Take 2-3 minutes each. Take notes and pray for each other's action steps during the week. As always, keep everything confidential.

In light of today's discussion, what is one step you can take in your life or in your relationships this week? Something specific. Something measurable. Something the group can pray for during the week.

Closing Prayer
Ask for God's guidance and strength during the week ahead.

NIEL - DEADLINES & BUSY WEEK

BILL - GOAL FINALIZING & LEADING TEAM IN THE PROCESS

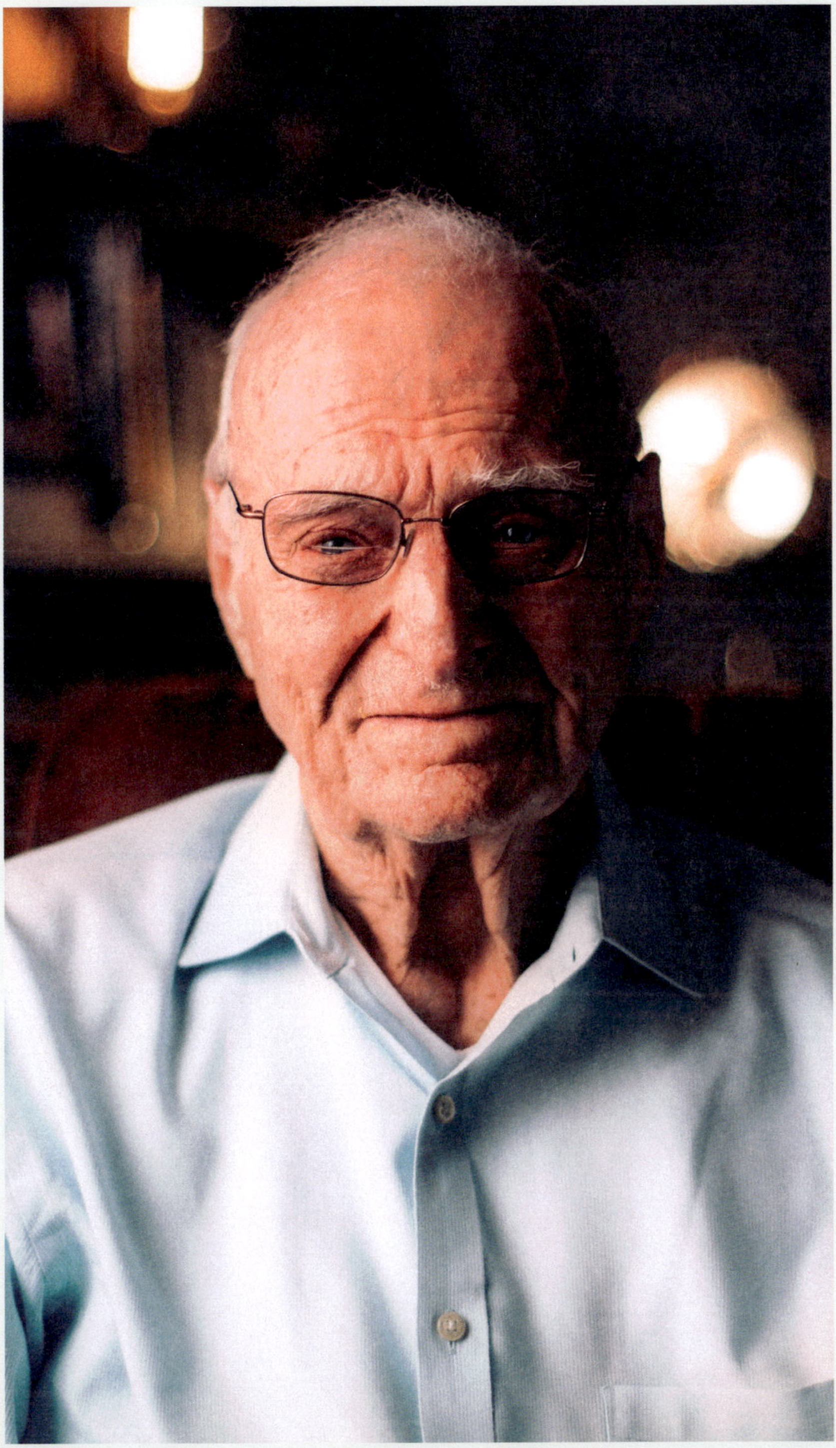

THE SECRET OF MAN'S BEING IS NOT ONLY TO LIVE – BUT TO LIVE FOR SOMETHING DEFINITE.

Fyodor Dostoyevsky

PERSONAL STUDY

EPISODE 5: TOM PATERSON - PURPOSE

Tom Patterson has lived an amazing life. He's experienced success, achievement and notoriety. He has also endured great tragedy, overwhelming loss, personal failure, addiction, and marital struggle - all this in one package.

Personal loss, tragedy, and failure do not disqualify you from being a vibrant participant in God's purpose for you.

Tom Paterson's protégé, Pete Richardson, mentions, "Most men lead lives of quiet desperation and die with the song still in their heart." That quote is usually attributed to author David Thoreau.

Here is Thoreau's full quote from the 1800's:

"The mass of men lead lives of quiet desperation. What is called resignation is confirmed desperation… A stereotyped but unconscious despair is concealed even under what are called the games and amusements of mankind."

Even though Thoreau said this over 150 years ago, it still rings true today.

God's calling pierces this nagging fear of desperation, isolation and meaninglessness. God has an overarching purpose for everyone. He also has a specific, unique calling and purpose for everyone, including you.

In Genesis, He states clearly that His intention is for us to collaborate with Him to be fruitful and multiply and subdue the earth (Genesis 1:28). The vision is to develop the social world and harness the natural world. The result God is after is universal flourishing. The amazing thing is that he wants to work through you to help others thrive.

God's original intent has been to collaborate with us in order to create cultures, build civilizations, and harness nature as we reflect His image of love, righteousness and goodness.

Our grand, overarching purpose is to collaborate with God and others to create flourishing, wholeness, and delight - in your personal life, your family life, your work life, your faith life, and your community life.

As Pete Richardson says,

"When I think you see the big picture of life from birth to death we realize how fast life is. Life is quick. It's swift. It's a blade of grass - green today, brown tomorrow - blown away by the wind the day after. To see your life as a gift and to begin to live day in and day out in a way that lives out of gratitude for that gift - and using your giftedness to make the world better in some way - I think that's purpose."

You have your story. Those in your CORE group have their story. But, your story does not define you. As Pete says,

"The thing with story is that any good story has its pinnacle times of great happiness and everything is going well and then deep dark valleys of hopelessness. The human story can be paralyzing if certain dots aren't connected. I know in my own story, some events in my life felt like outliers. They felt like disconnected, unmeaningful episodes... many of which I wish I could have deleted or erased. But what I discovered is that there's never a meaningless experience or episode in your life."

The reason for this is that God redeems the losses and failures for His purposes, if we allow Him. He uses our seasons of sorrow to bring us closer to Him, His grace, and His mercy. The second beatitude says, *"blessed are they who mourn, for they will be comforted"* **(Matthew 5:4)**. Pain and suffering can either drive us away from God as we seek to disconnect from the pain through addictions and distractions, or it can draw us closer to God, as we pursue His comfort, His grace, and His mercy.

CHOOSING TO REST IN HIS GRACE AND MERCY IS A PATH THAT ULTIMATELY LEADS TO A NEW PERSPECTIVE, JOY AND RESTORATION. IT IS IN THIS TRANSFORMATIONAL PROCESS THAT OUR SPECIFIC CALLING AND PURPOSE CAN BE REFINED. THE FOUNDATION OF THIS IS BEING FREED FROM GUILT AND SHAME AND BECOMING CONFIDENT IN WHAT GOD BELIEVES IS TRUE ABOUT US.

Pete mentions how Jesus began his ministry on earth with His Father affirming that he loves him and is pleased with him. And in the same way, the scriptures address how we are to get settled with the truth that,

"... you received God's Spirit when he adopted you as his own children. Now we call him, "Abba, Father." For his Spirit joins with our spirit to affirm that we are God's children." **Romans 8:15-16 (NLT)**

One of the primary works of the Holy Spirit in our lives is to affirm that we are beloved sons. Only when we understand the truth that not only have we been forgiven, but that we are adopted and empowered sons, will we stop seeking the false idols of the broken male culture to give us satisfaction. This is as big a battle as you will ever face in your life. That's why we need the help of brothers to help remind us of who we really are and what we were made for.

Brotherhood is a primary component in working your way through the fog of uncertainty. As Pete unpacks in the film, "There is power in a well-timed question, that cuts through all the fog and allows the good, bad, and ugly around that question to come out and be made visible. It's hard to do this alone. It's because we need help. We need brothers, friends who believe deeply in us and are willing to listen and are curious about what's wrong. What's confused? What's missing? Where am I failing? Where am I succeeding? And they give us hope. Otherwise, all there is, is judgment. We don't need more judgment. We judge ourselves harshly enough. Sometimes just getting that stuff out of my head and heart begins to bring hope in a bizarre way."

Clarifying your specific purpose is an ongoing unveiling. Interaction within your group can help pierce the fog of subjectivity that we all have (1 Corinthians 13:12) through the input and example of others. We also need others to encourage us when we can't see the impact our lives are having or could have. They help us see God's hand as He guides us out of the wildernesses of our own making.

The key is to be willing to step out of the familiar and into new expressions of serving others. Become open to this grand calling. Be curious about what God has been preparing you for. Be intentional to put yourself in opportunities to create flourishing for others. They may not seem like grand, earth shaking arenas. Just be willing to step out. God knows how to direct and redirect you as long as you are moving. He will hone your awareness of new ways you can contribute to the magnificent vision of his Kingdom come, his will be done, on earth as it is in heaven.

EPISODE 5
REFLECTION

PERSONAL STUDY QUESTIONS

1. What are you clear about right now regarding God's purpose for you in your life?

2. Specifically, what areas of flourishing in the world and your life are you currently called to? What are you passionate about? What do you love? How have you seen God use you?

3. Have I addressed my Action step that I shared with my CORE Group? If not, what is keeping me from stepping out and addressing it? What's my next step?

JOURNALING:

Write your answers in your notebook. Also, journal about what comes to mind that can be applied to the specific areas in your life you are committed to taking new ground, as What are referenced in your vision you created in Session 1. you learning? What is happening? Where are you making progress? Where are you stuck? What's working? What's not working? What's wanted and needed? What's next?

Go to coreunites.com/quiz to assess where you are in your path to finding purpose and identity.

SCRIPTURE REFLECTION:

We encourage you to consider this following scripture passage over the course of this week in a contemplative way. Read the passage four separate times. It works well if you read it on four separate days. Each time you read it, read it from a different perspective.

1. With the first reading, be alert for a phrase or word that stands out for you.

2. During the second reading, take a moment to reflect on what touches you, perhaps saying that particular verse out loud or writing it in your notebook.

3. After reading the passage a third time, respond with a prayer to God about what you have experienced and what the scripture might be calling you to.

4. Finally, rest in silence after a fourth reading, trusting that, *"it is God who works in you, both to will and to work for his good pleasure."* **Philippians 2:13 (ESV)**

This process helps you to engage not only your mind, but your heart and soul in worshipful reflection on the scriptures. This can also give you fresh courage and trust to take new ground to where God is calling you forward.

Here is this week's reflection scripture: **PSALMS 138:1-3, 7-8 (ESV)**

I give you thanks, O Lord, with my whole heart; before the gods I sing your praise; I bow down toward your holy temple and give thanks to your name for your steadfast love and your faithfulness, for you have exalted above all things your name and your word. On the day I called, you answered me; my strength of soul you increased.

Though I walk in the midst of trouble, you preserve my life; you stretch out your hand against the wrath of my enemies, and your right hand delivers me. The Lord will fulfill his purpose for me; your steadfast love, O Lord, endures forever.

- THERE IS POWER IN A WELL TIMED QUESTION THAT CUTS THROUGH ALL THE FOG

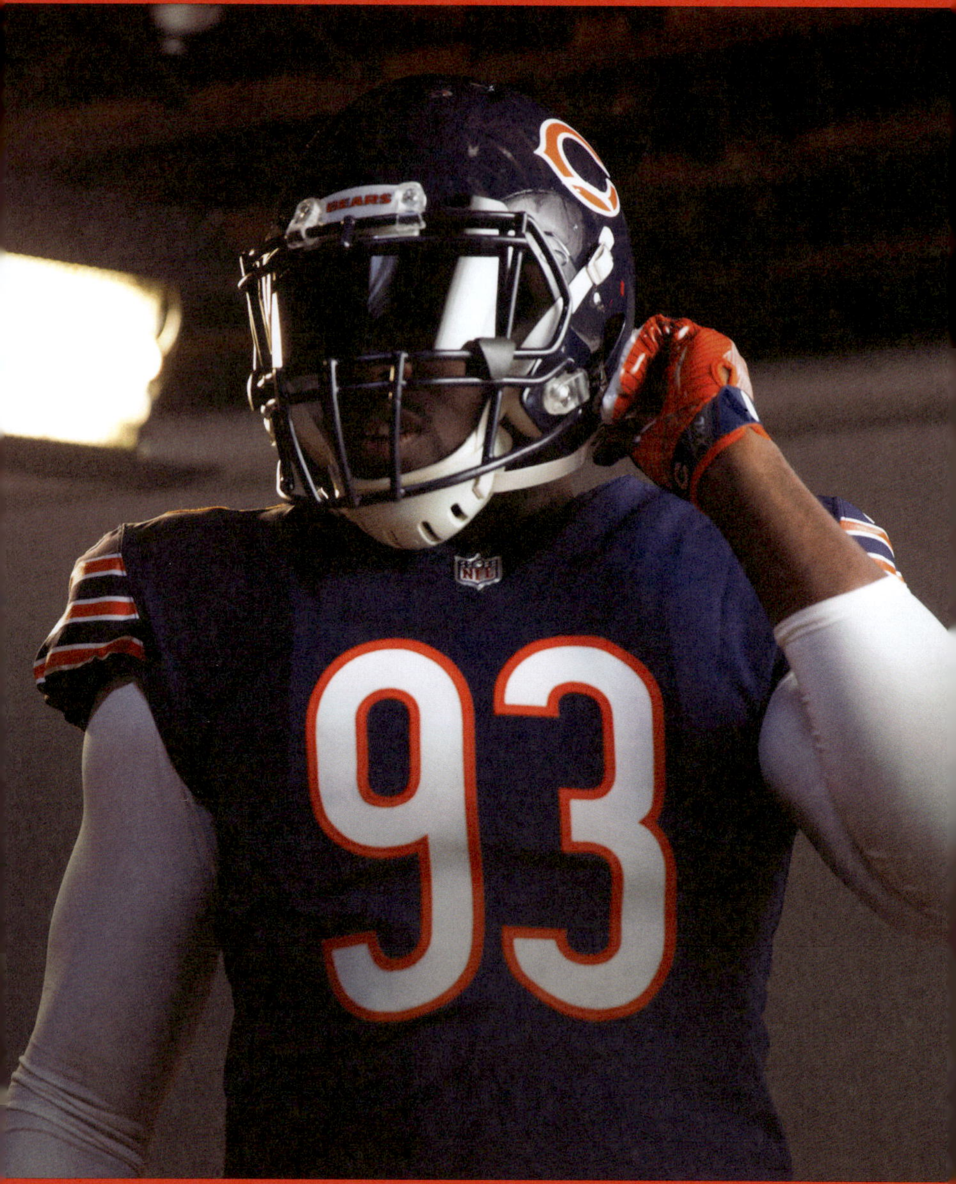
BEARS
93

EPISODE

6

THE ACHOS BROTHERHOOD

GROUP DISCUSSION GUIDE
90 MINUTES

Opening Prayer
Surrender time and heart to God's leading.

Check In (25 minutes)
1. How has your week gone? Family? Work?
2. What kind of progress or challenges did you have with your Action step?
3. How was your Personal Study and Scripture Reflection time this week? What is resonating? What is not working?

Check In time is high on encouragement and low on "accountability".

Watch Film (10 minutes)
Acho Brothers - Brotherhood

Discussion (45 minutes)
1. What part of the Acho's story did you connect with?
2. Sam said he regrets not opening up to his brother about the things he messed up in. What are the reasons we have that keep us from opening up to those close to us?
3. What can we do as a group to increase the level of authenticity and connection with each other?

Action (10 minutes)
Be mindful of the need for everyone to have an opportunity to talk. Take 2-3 minutes each. Take notes and pray for each other's action steps during the week. As always, keep everything confidential.

In light of today's discussion, what is one step you can take in your life or in your relationships this week? Something specific. Something measurable. Something the group can pray for during the week.

Closing Prayer
Ask for God's guidance and strength during the week ahead. Remember to pray for the guys in your group this week.

PERSONAL STUDY

EPISODE 6: ACHO BROTHERS - BROTHERHOOD

Your CORE group is designed to help facilitate a "brotherhood" connection with those in your group. This group serves as an opportunity to be completely open and honest. It is a relationship committed to addressing issues that can have a significant impact on your life and those around you.

What's the number one quality you want in your CORE group? It's not common life stage. Not common education. Not common economic status. Not common ethnicity. Not common political bias. Not common spiritual maturity. Then what is it? Common purpose! Are you all after the same thing?

If you have the same ultimate goal, then the other differences actually work for you. They give you different perspectives to help one another achieve the same end goal. There was a reason Jesus picked men from vastly different backgrounds. Do you think Matthew, the sell-out tax collector and Simon the anti-tax zealot had some interesting water cooler conversations? It certainly wasn't a political alliance that created their common bond.

What they had in common was a willingness to pay a price to follow Jesus. A willingness to be challenged to the core of their old identities and loyalties to share their singular most important identity – being followers of Jesus. They had lots of hang-ups and self-interests. But this singular common commitment made them a formidable group. One that the greatest powers on earth could not and would not stop.

Are you willing to share the good, the bad, and the ugly in order to help your CORE group overcome old ways and beliefs? To be open to embrace one another's vulnerabilities with encouragement and grace?

It takes courage to be real, rather than trying to mask with half-truths, denial, minimizing or lying. It creates an intimacy and connection that enables you to share what causes suffering in your life and what you are challenged with. We all have that. Vulnerability can be life giving to be able to share with others who get it.

> **'BROTHERHOOD' IS ONE OF THE GREATEST ENVIRONMENTS TO EXPERIENCE THE KIND OF TRANSFORMATION YOU DESIRE.**

In the film, Sam shares a regret in his relationship with his brother: "I've missed the boat, in my opinion, in being Emmanuel's brother, for example, his relationships with women - and even in my mistakes, I didn't really share that with him because if I jacked up, made a mistake and know he knows, that might give him permission to do the same. So, I most wanted to maintain this perception of being a perfect older brother - which probably hurt him more than helped him."

MY BEST FRIEND IS THE ONE WHO BRINGS OUT THE BEST IN ME.

Henry Ford

"In my mind, the only way an example would be helpful is if it was perfect. I wanted him to think I have it all together and you can have it all together, too. Which no one does. There's nobody in the world who does. But I wanted him to view it that way. I think if I would have been more transparent with him about my failures and my struggles and stuff that I'm going through daily, it probably would have helped him more. The reality is that I'm still trying to figure out Sam (who I am)."

Sam goes on to say, "Just be yourself, stop trying to fit into this situation or that situation and be liked by these guys or by those guys or be cool, look cool and just be who you are. I love the fact that he and I have such a close relationship, because not a lot of brothers have that. I don't feel like I have to hide or pretend. I live and die for relationships. It's like my brother coming to Chicago to hang out with me or me going to Austin and us kicking it. He's more reserved, just let him do his thing on his phone, and I'm like, hey, tell me about your life. Tell me about this girl you've been dating. Tell me about football. Tell me about what's going on. What is God teaching you?"

Consider this question. When you heard Sam share how he hid some things from his brother, did you think less of him? His honesty was refreshing to hear, wasn't it? For the vast majority of us, not only did we not think less of Sam, but we actually appreciated him more! Why is that? Because there is something very powerful when a brother is willing to open up about personal weakness with the hope to overcome. It brings the best out of us on so many levels.

Just like each of us, Sam and Emmanuel are learning the dynamics of true brotherhood. While they are brothers from the same family, these dynamics hold true for all friendships, whether related by blood or not.

Your CORE group might be a God-given opportunity for you to begin trusting one another with issues that you've been struggling to figure out on your own. It is up to you though. It will take an act of courage to lay yourself bare like this. It is your choice. If you don't think it wise to discuss an issue with the entire group, then consider who in the group you can share it with.

'Brotherhood' is one of the greatest environments to experience the kind of transformation you dream of. It is designed to help free us from self-centered, isolated, secret living. **It is in brotherhood that you can learn one of the most powerful and life-giving experiences – wanting someone else's breakthrough to be as important to you as if it were your own.** It's what Jesus modeled for us. It is how we were originally designed to live.

Our culture is so isolating. The isolation that most live in is suffocating. It breeds desperation and hopelessness, a toxic combination. The belief that others aren't struggling with similar issues makes us want to lie and hide our true selves. In our culture we are trained to speak as if we are confident, thriving and healthy. Yet underneath the surface we know that we often aren't those things. We need to know others and be known by others, but we rarely know how to do that. Ralph Waldo Emerson said,

"The glory of friendship is not the outstretched hand, nor the kindly smile, nor the joy of companionship. It is the spiritual inspiration that comes to one when he discovers that someone else believes in him and is willing to trust him."

Your CORE Group Dynamics are designed to create a deep sense of friendship with each other over time. It doesn't happen overnight. And our hope and prayer is that your group continues beyond the ten weeks of this particular foundational series.

Make the practice of 'brotherhood' a mainstay in your life.

A very simple way to go deeper with this is to follow the CORE group guidelines. Go back to the beginning of this Participant Guide and review the CORE Group Dynamics section at the front of this book. Think of these methods as ways of being with each other that create opportunities to be real and connect so that you can help one another experience personal breakthroughs. This is one of the ultimate expressions of love,

"Love is unselfishly choosing for another's highest good." C.S. Lewis

EPISODE 6
REFLECTION

PERSONAL STUDY QUESTIONS

1. What are you currently struggling with and what would you like to invite your CORE group to support you in?
2. Where can you be more effective in supporting your CORE group?
3. Have I addressed my Action step that I shared with my CORE Group? If not, what is keeping me from stepping out and addressing it? What's my next step?

JOURNALING:

Write your answers in your notebook. What are you learning? What is happening? Where are you making progress? Where are you stuck?

What's working? What's not working? What's wanted and needed? What's next?

SCRIPTURE REFLECTION:

We encourage you to consider this following scripture passage over the course of this week in a contemplative way. Read the passage four separate times. It works well if you read it on four separate days. Each time you read it, read it from a different perspective.

1. With the first reading, be alert for a phrase or word that stands out for you.

2. During the second reading, take a moment to reflect on what touches you, perhaps saying that particular verse out loud or writing it in your notebook.

3. After reading the passage a third time, respond with a prayer to God about what you have experienced and what the scripture might be calling you to.

4. Finally, rest in silence after a fourth reading, trusting that, *"it is God who works in you, both to will and to work for his good pleasure."* **Philippians 2:13 (ESV)**

This process helps you to engage not only your mind, but your heart and soul in worshipful reflection on the scriptures. This can also give you fresh courage and trust to take new ground to where God is calling you forward.

This week's reflection scripture: **PHILIPPIANS 1:27-2:2 (ESV)**

Only let your manner of life be worthy of the gospel of Christ, so that whether I come and see you or am absent, I may hear of you that you are standing firm in one spirit, with one mind striving side by side for the faith of the gospel, and not frightened in anything by your opponents.

This is a clear sign to them of their destruction, but of your salvation, and that from God. For it has been granted to you that for the sake of Christ you should not only believe in him but also suffer for his sake, engaged in the same conflict that you saw I had and now hear that I still have.

So if there is any encouragement in Christ, any comfort from love, any participation in the Spirit, any affection and sympathy, complete my joy by being of the same mind, having the same love, being in full accord and of one mind.

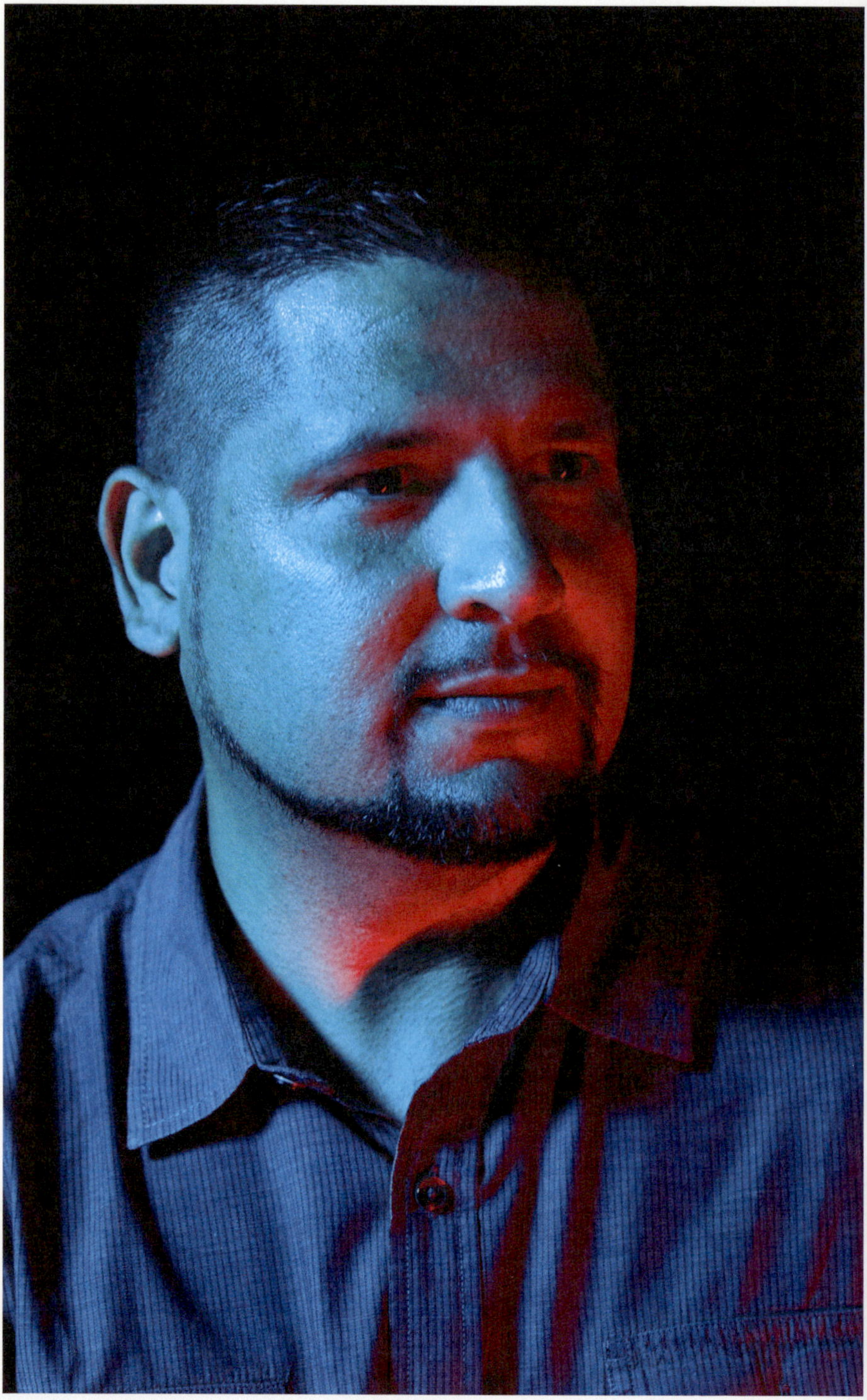

EPISODE

7

JERRY QUIROZ
CHOICES

GROUP DISCUSSION GUIDE
90 MINUTES

Opening Prayer
Surrender time and heart to God's leading.

Check In (25 minutes)
Be mindful that you are not taking more time to talk than the others in the group.

1. How has your week gone? Family? Work?

2. What kind of progress or challenges did you have with your Action step?

3. How was your Personal Study and Scripture Reflection time this week? What is resonating? What is not working?

No judgment zone. Remember that we are here to listen. Consider, how can I understand and encourage?

Watch Film (10 minutes)
Jerry Quiroz - Choices

Discussion (45 minutes)
1. What part of Jerry's story did you connect with?

2. What hard decisions are you currently facing? What do you need to help you with this?

Action (10 minutes)
In light of today's discussion, what is one step you can take in your life or in your relationships this week? Something specific. Something measurable. Something the group can pray for during the week.

Be mindful of the need for everyone to have an opportunity to talk. Take 2-3 minutes each. Take notes and pray for each other's action steps during the week. As always, keep everything confidential.

Closing Prayer
Ask for God's guidance and strength during the week ahead. Remember to pray during the week for your group and the decisions they are wanting to make.

PERSONAL STUDY

EPISODE 7: JERRY QUIROZ - CHOICES

Jerry's story is a story of grace. Out of God's kindness and His love, He intervened while Jerry rebelled. This is what God does. It's the story of the Gospel. Even though we haven't deserved it, God already has a plan in place to save us from ourselves. Life can get messy, but in Jerry's story we see that God's passion is to rescue us by providing an alternative.

Have you gotten to a place where you've given up hope that God will ever change some part of you? Is there some insecurity, temperament, or behavior that, at this point, you're just so accustomed to, that you're now convinced "this is just who I am"?

God transforms people. You are never too old, too rebellious, or too hopeless for God to do so. This is one of the most consistent narratives in the entire Bible. He transforms people. He gives us new longings. He gives us new desires. He changes our heart which changes the way we live. Whatever your story is, our hope is that you see that God has the desire and the power to change you.

We cannot emphasize enough that those in your CORE group are a valuable resource in this. Jerry's friend, Nathan, was that to him. In the film, Jerry recounts after he confessed his lying and cheating to his wife,

"I felt like everything that was holding us just got torn. And I prayed to God and I said, God you told me to say these things so now, where are you? For my marriage, this was the lowest point. I went to seek help at our church and our young adult ministry pastor, Nathan, was there. I let him know what just happened. Nathan was a great support during this difficult time. The love and forgiveness from God came through being around other men of God who imparted that identity in me. I found this allowed me to fully receive forgiveness as a son." This is the beauty of friendship.

We, like Jason Bourne, have let the wounds of life cause us to forget who we are. We need others to remind us who we really are. It's not about giving endless advice. It's not about judging. It's not about shaming. It's not about avoiding. It's not about minimizing or dismissing.

Instead it's about loving, being honest, transparent, real, and encouraging. We all struggle. To deny it is vanity and willful blindness. Having fellow wounded healers alongside us is how God rolls best.

Now, all of these descriptions of God's restorative work in our lives is energizing and refreshing. But you have a responsibility in this work. You must be willing to get real about your life, as it currently is. This is something we see in Jerry's story.

Jerry's life came to a crossroads. God opened his eyes so that Jerry could see how his dream of becoming a star soccer player had become a self-destructive idol.

Tim Keller gives some helpful insight, **"What is an idol? It is anything more important to you than God, anything that absorbs our heart and imagination more than God,**

RESCUE IS THE CONSTANT PATTERN OF GOD'S ACTIVITY.

Francis Frangipane

anything you seek to give you what only God can give."

Anything can become an idol for us. Sometimes, an idol is a good thing that becomes the main thing. Success can certainly be an idol. Attaining wealth can become an idol. Power in relationships can become an idol.

Success, wealth and power can all be good things, until they become the one thing. They are not automatically an idol. It is how you relate to them that determines whether you have them or if they have you.

Keller adds this, "Contemporary idol worship continues today in the form of an addiction or devotion to money, career, sex, power and anything people seek to give significance and satisfaction in life other than God."

Let's look at some of what God has to say about idols,

"All who fashion idols are nothing, and the things they delight in do not profit. Their witnesses neither see nor know, that they may be put to shame. Who fashions a god or casts an idol that is profitable for nothing? Behold, all his companions shall be put to shame, and the craftsmen are only human. Let them all assemble, let them stand forth. They shall be terrified; they shall be put to shame together."
Isaiah 44:9-11 (ESV)

Anything you put your trust in to carry the day, other than God, is becoming a functioning idol to you. Idols aren't typically in and of themselves "bad things". It's when anything in your life other than God becomes the "ultimate thing".

- Success can become an idol.
- Money can become an idol.
- Sexual gratification can become an idol.
- Being right can become an idol.
- Looking good can become an idol.
- Comfort can become an idol.
- Being in control can become an idol.

And on and on it goes... the list of possible idols seems endless.

So, what does the scripture above in Isaiah tell us are the ramifications of relying on idols?

- If we fashion idols, we are nothing. We are producing nothing worthwhile.
- We will reap no profit.
- We will experience shame.
- We will experience fear. In fact, we will be driven by fear.

Jerry loved soccer. He was good at soccer. He enjoyed soccer. Is soccer in and of itself a bad thing? Not at all. But for Jerry success in soccer became all that really mattered to him. His thoughts and hopes were built around soccer. If you had asked him at the time if that were true, he might have denied it. But the way he was living revealed the reality of his idolatry and the destructive impact it was having on his wife.

His wife's commitment to their marriage was a catalyst for Jerry to start looking at things from a different perspective. And he realized that, for him, the wise choice was to go in a completely different direction. This is what the word "repent" means. It means to change your trajectory.

Jerry made the choices he needed to make to change his trajectory. And, in doing so, he is completely transforming the legacy of his life.

WE HAVE A CHOICE... MOMENT-BY-MOMENT, DAY-BY-DAY. WE CHOOSE.

Jesus' first instructions to his followers were to *"repent, for the kingdom of heaven is at hand."* **(Matthew 3:2)** What he meant was to change your focus, change what matters most to you, change the trajectory you are on. Why do that? Because "the kingdom of heaven is at hand." Because making this commitment, an act of the will, opens up the fullness of what God has for us. It's the path to living in freedom, no longer weighed down by guilt and shame. It's the path He has prepared in all His wisdom and guidance, rather than us just blindly following our desires and notions.

We have a choice - moment by moment, day by day. We choose. Deuteronomy so vividly encapsulates that choice.

"I call heaven and earth to testify against you today! I've set life and death before you today: both blessings and curses. Choose life, that it may be well with you—you and your children"
DEUTERONOMY 30:19 (ISV)

God's path leads to life - the fullness of life. All else pales in comparison, and ultimately leads to death. The choice is yours. Don't go it alone. You may stumble. If you do, pick yourself up and go again. Moment by moment, we choose. And those choices determine the trajectory of your life.

EPISODE 7
REFLECTION

PERSONAL STUDY QUESTIONS

1. What choices do you need to make today, at this point in time, to move you towards God's plan for your life?
2. Who in your life is living in such a way that you can gain inspiration and strength for your own journey? How can you engage them in a more purposeful and intentional way?
3. Have I addressed my Action step that I shared with my CORE Group? If not, what is keeping me from stepping out and addressing it? What's my next step?

JOURNALING:

Write your answers in your notebook. Also, journal about what comes to mind that can be applied to the specific areas in your life you are committed to taking new ground, as referenced in your vision you created in Session 1. What are you learning? What is happening? Where are you making progress? Where are you stuck? What's working? What's not working? What's wanted and needed? What's next?

SCRIPTURE REFLECTION:

We encourage you to consider this following scripture passage over the course of this week in a contemplative way. Read the passage four separate times. It works well if you read it on four separate days. Each time you read it, read it from a different perspective.

1. With the first reading, be alert for a phrase or word that stands out for you.
2. During the second reading, take a moment to reflect on what touches you, perhaps saying that particular verse out loud or writing it in your notebook.
3. After reading the passage a third time, respond with a prayer to God about what you have experienced and what the scripture might be calling you to.
4. Finally, rest in silence after a fourth reading, trusting that, *"it is God who works in you, both to will and to work for his good pleasure."* **Philippians 2:13 (ESV)**

This process helps you to engage not only your mind, but your heart and soul in worshipful reflection on the scriptures. This can also give you fresh courage and trust to take new ground to where God is calling you forward.

This week's reflection scripture: **1 PETER 2:9-11 (NIV)**

But you are a chosen people, a royal priesthood, a holy nation, God's special possession, that you may declare the praises of him who called you out of darkness into his wonderful light. Once you were not a people, but now you are the people of God; once you had not received mercy, but now you have received mercy. Dear friends, I urge you, as foreigners and exiles, to abstain from sinful desires, which wage war against your soul.

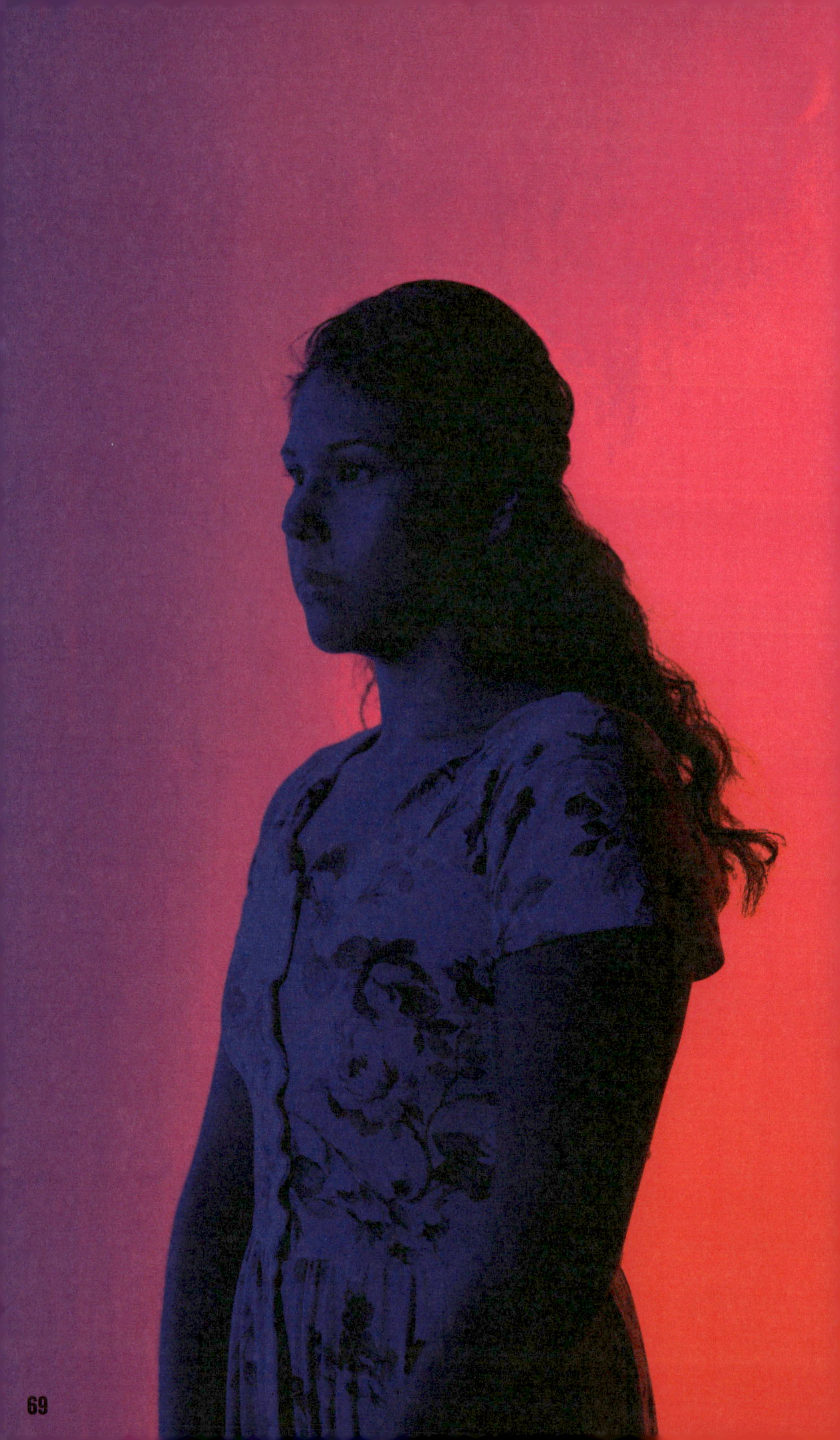

70

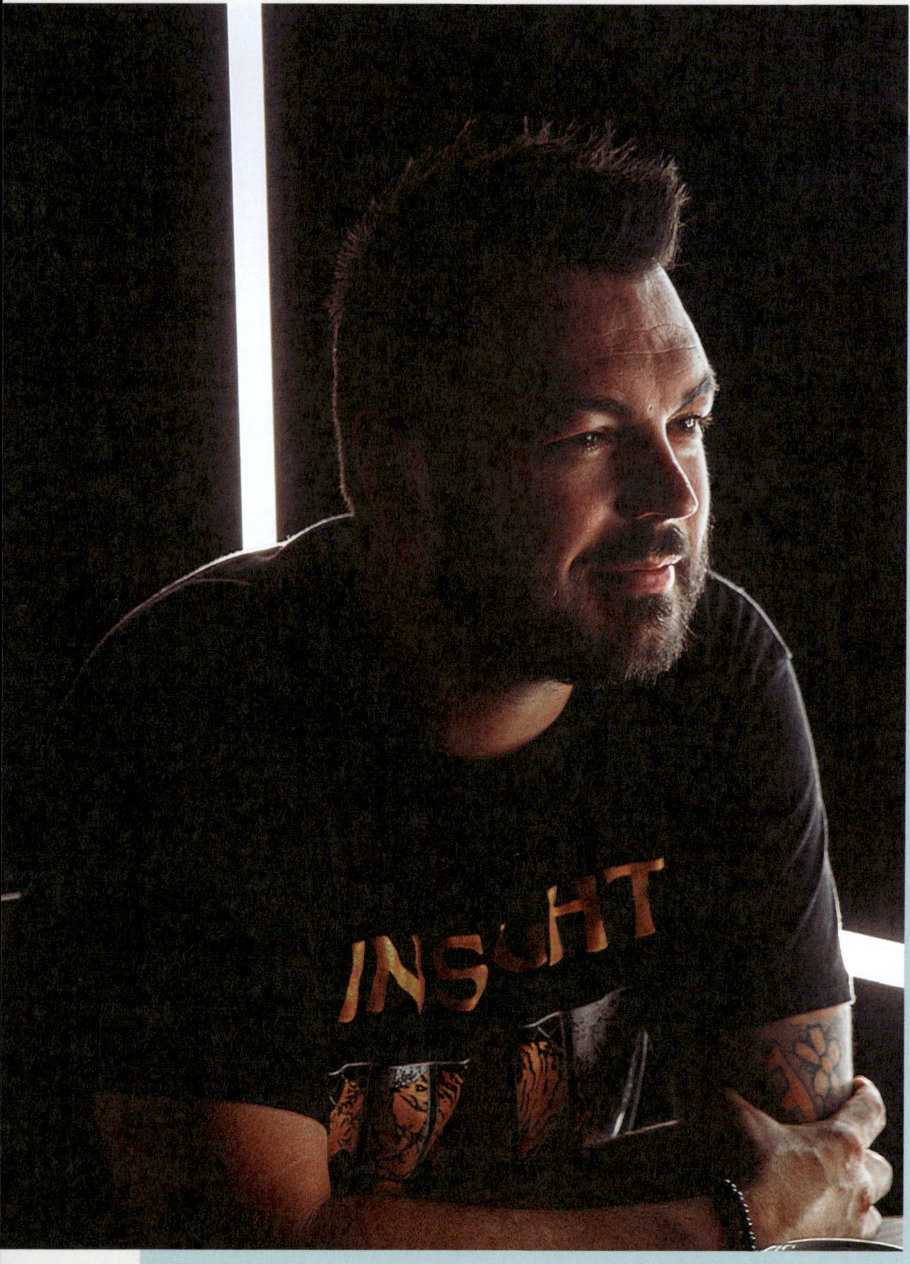

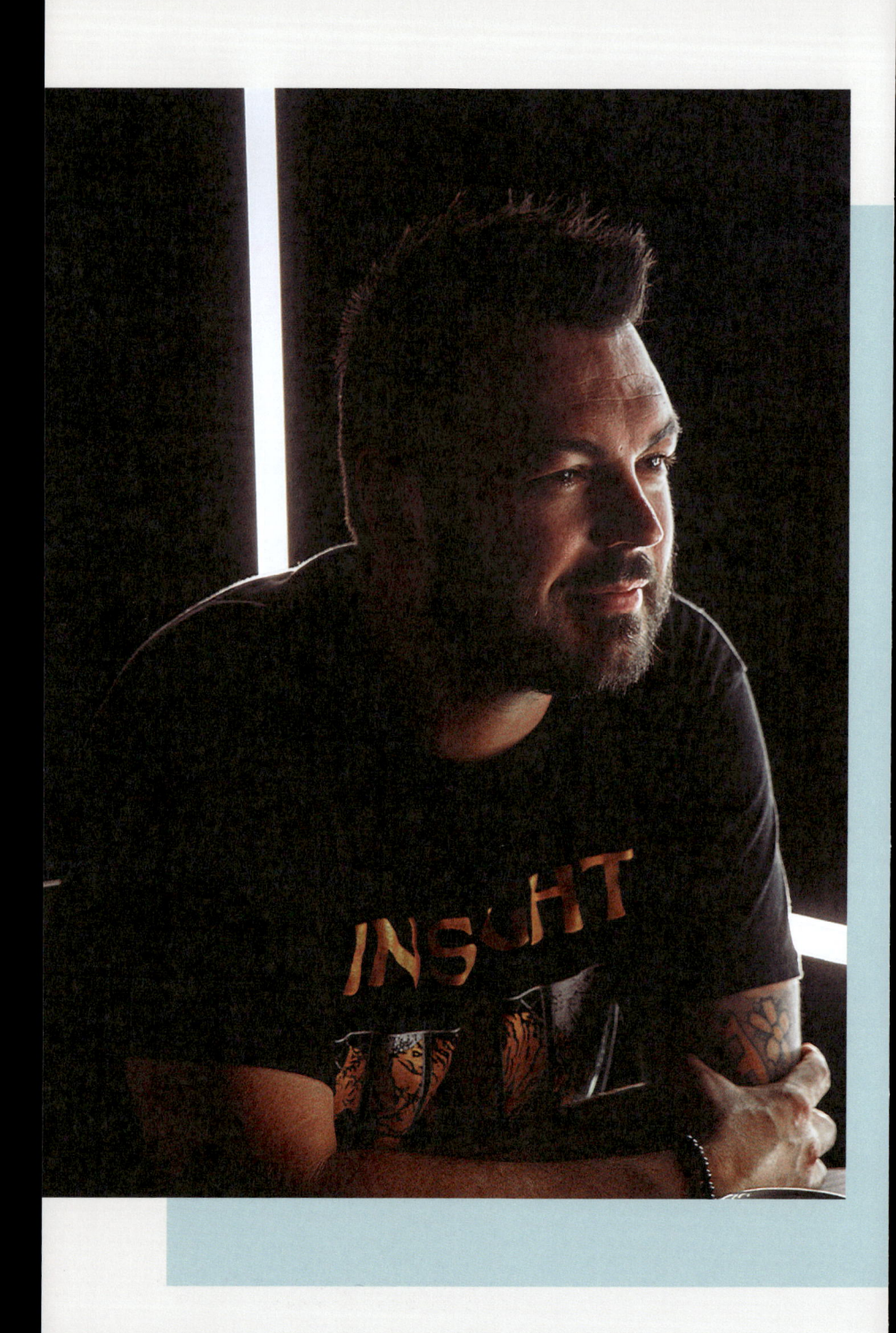

EPISODE 8

TOMMY GREEN
PAIN

GROUP DISCUSSION GUIDE
90 MINUTES

Opening Prayer
Surrender time and heart to God's leading.

Check In (25 minutes)
Be mindful that you are not taking more time to talk than the others in the group.
1. How has your week gone? Family? Work?
2. What kind of progress or challenges did you have with your Action step?
3. How was your Personal Study and Scripture Reflection time this week? What is resonating? What is not working?

No judgment zone. Remember that we are here to listen. Consider, how can I understand and encourage?

Watch Film (10 minutes)
Tommy Green - Pain

Discussion (45 minutes)
1. What part of Tommy's story did you connect with?
2. How do you think your father would answer your question, "How do you feel about me?"
3. Have you ever felt the necessity to pursue or reconcile with someone when you knew there was little chance for reciprocation? What happened when you did or did not follow through with it?

Action (10 minutes)
In light of today's discussion, what is one step you can take in your life or in your relationships this week? Something specific. Something measurable. Something the group can pray for during the week.

Be mindful of the need for everyone to have an opportunity to talk. Take 2-3 minutes each. Take notes and pray for each other's action steps during the week. As always, keep everything confidential.

Closing Prayer
Ask for God's guidance and strength during the week ahead.

PERSONAL STUDY

EPISODE 8: TOMMY GREEN - PAIN

Tommy Green's story is intense and sobering.

It's the story of one man's struggle with the ongoing impact of a father's anger and abuse. It is about a man who desired to become free from his rage and inner doubts, and ultimately becoming an agent of healing in his culture.

What is Tommy's vision for himself and the young people that listen to his music? He tells us, "Hopefully, I've become a father in an orphaned culture."

Tommy is in the process of transforming the pain of his father's abuse into a passion for being a father to a fatherless generation. He sought and found an outlet to stay real and still have that authenticity be a form of worship instead of destruction.

NO MATTER THE CIRCUMSTANCE, YOU CAN TRUST IN YOUR HEAVENLY FATHER'S CHARACTER. HE TRULY IS ALWAYS TRUSTWORTHY.

In the film, Tommy said.

"I had fury as a son and I had deep loss and rejection with nowhere to put it."

"Fire…if you put it in the right thing it can warm the house, right? If you just let it go, it'll burn the house down. So, I felt like this (his music) can be like my fire. I can put all that I'm feeling in this thing and it can go somewhere. It gave my absolute rage and abandonment towards my father, towards my stepfather, towards this whole planet, towards God… I could put all of it in context. And I knew other people felt like me. It gave my pain a voice in that."

"When I met Jesus for real, I just wanted to create worship that made sense to me that wouldn't alienate my culture, but at the same time would build a bridge so that eventually people could worship together."

"We did a show in Southern California. I remember it was with a whole bunch of kids and I remember it was in San Bernardino on Father's Day. There was like 5,000 people. And I remember going 'yeah, there's 5,000 dudes here at this show not with their dads.' So, we are ministering to a gaping wound in a generation…that cycle of fatherlessness…that hunger… that void that isn't quite met is the root of all sorts of dysfunction and sorrow and pain."

Tommy has taken the abandonment and rage that he felt and has seen God redeem it. Instead of being ruled by it - these deep emotions have become an offering of thanks to God for the new identity he has given us all…to be HIS CHILDREN. Our choice is to rage against the unfairness of the world we were born into or to embrace the path of sonship that God has freely offered us.

Some of these verses were addressed earlier but their brilliance is worth repeating,

Romans 8:14-17 (ESV) *For all who are led by the Spirit of God are sons of God. For you did not receive the spirit of slavery to fall back into fear, but you have received the Spirit of adoption as sons, by*

C.S. Lewis

FATHERHOOD MUST BE AT THE CORE OF THE UNIVERSE BECAUSE THE CREATOR OF THE UNIVERSE IS HIMSELF A FATHER.

whom we cry, "Abba! Father!" The Spirit himself bears witness with our spirit that we are children of God, and if children, then heirs—heirs of God and fellow heirs with Christ, provided we suffer with him in order that we may also be glorified with him.

The phrase "Abba Father" is interesting. "Abba" is an Aramaic word most closely related to the word "daddy" today. Jesus opened the path for us to have a deeply intimate relationship with God, our Father. But He is not some distant authority figure that is inaccessible to us. He is our Daddy. He desires intimacy with us. He wants to hold us close to his heart and shower us with his love.

Fatherlessness is an ongoing, catastrophic crisis in our culture today. The only sure solution for this is to embrace God as our "Abba father" – our Daddy. To embrace His love, grace and mercy towards us. He tells us He will never leave us or forsake us **(Hebrews 13:5).**

As humans, we are weak and fall short. As the God of the universe, He is strong and reliable. Even when it looks like nothing is working, He is still there.

How was your relationship with your father? Even if you never met him (which would also impact you). You might have the closest of relationships with your father, or you might only know him by his absence. The impact of your father is significant, for better or for worse,

"Fathers interpret life for their children – give life structure and meaning. They do so whether they mean to or not. It either becomes the foundation on which we build a life, or the rubble we dig out from under." Gary Stanley

No father is perfect. Most are far from perfect. How you relate to your father's imperfections influence much of your life. Tommy Green eventually saw that fully embracing the love extended to him by his heavenly Father was the key to transforming his way of relating to the rejection of his earthly father. Tommy's trust in the true Fatherhood of God has moved him from rage to redemption.

If Christ is your Savior, then God is your Father. He invites you into an intimate relationship with Him. He will never leave you or forsake you. He is good, even in the worst of times. No matter the circumstance, you can trust in your Heavenly Father's character. As we addressed in an earlier film, He truly is always trustworthy to take our broken things and make something beautiful out of them. Tommy's life illustrates this.

Leaning into this reality and allowing it to heal you from the wounds of your past is the key to not paying the rage forward. It can heal your fury while moving you towards forgiveness, love, joy, peace, forbearance, kindness, goodness, faithfulness, gentleness and self-control **(Galatians 5:22)**.

This takes time. It takes obedience. It takes a commitment to grow and change. And, most of all, it takes trusting God that He is who He says He is and He will do what He says He will do.

It's worth the risk. Your legacy hangs in the balance before you.

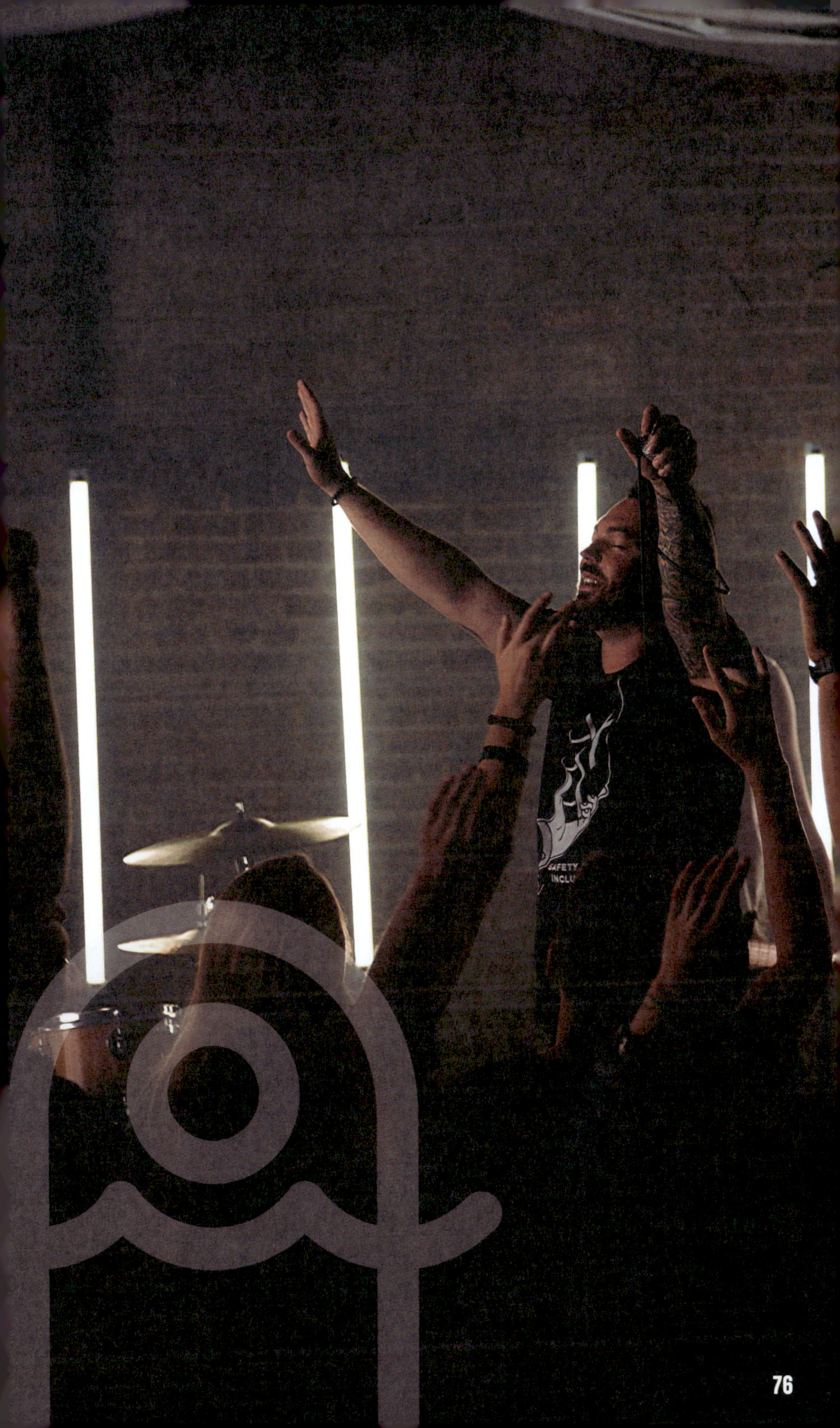

EPISODE 8
REFLECTION

PERSONAL STUDY QUESTIONS

1. What was missing for you in your relationship with your father? Even if you have or had a great relationship with your dad, no father is perfect. What was missing for you?
2. How does that influence your relationship with God as your Father?
3. Have I addressed my Action step that I shared with my CORE Group? If not, what is keeping me from stepping out and addressing it? What's my next step?

JOURNALING:

Write your answers in your notebook. Also, journal about what comes to mind that can be applied to the specific areas in your life you are committed to taking new ground, as referenced in your vision you created in Session 1. What are you learning? What is happening? Where are you making progress? Where are you stuck? What's working? What's not working? What's wanted and needed? What's next?

SCRIPTURE REFLECTION:

We encourage you to consider this following scripture passage over the course of this week in a contemplative way. Read the passage four separate times. It works well if you read it on four separate days. Each time you read it, read it from a different perspective.

1. With the first reading, be alert for a phrase or word that stands out for you.
2. During the second reading, take a moment to reflect on what touches you, perhaps saying that particular verse out loud or writing it in your notebook.
3. After reading the passage a third time, respond with a prayer to God about what you have experienced and what the scripture might be calling you to.
4. Finally, rest in silence after a fourth reading, trusting that, *"it is God who works in you, both to will and to work for his good pleasure."* **Philippians 2:13 (ESV)**

This process helps you to engage not only your mind, but your heart and soul in worshipful reflection on the scriptures. This can also give you fresh courage and trust to take new ground to where God is calling you forward.

This week's reflection scripture: **ROMANS 8:12-17 (ESV)**

So then, brothers, we are debtors, not to the flesh, to live according to the flesh. For if you live according to the flesh you will die, but if by the Spirit you put to death the deeds of the body, you will live.

For all who are led by the Spirit of God are sons of God. For you did not receive the spirit of slavery to fall back into fear, but you have received the Spirit of adoption as sons, by whom we cry, "Abba! Father!"

The Spirit himself bears witness with our spirit that we are children of God, and if children, then heirs—heirs of God and fellow heirs with Christ, provided we suffer with him in order that we may also be glorified with him.

EPISODE 9

PROPAGANDA
IDENTITY

GROUP DISCUSSION GUIDE
90 MINUTES

Opening Prayer
Surrender time and heart to God's leading.

Check In (25 minutes)
Be mindful that you are not taking more time to talk than the others in the group.

1. How has your week gone? Family? Work?
2. What kind of progress or challenges did you have with your Action step?
3. How was your Personal Study and Scripture Reflection time this week? What is resonating? What is not working?

No judgment zone. Remember that we are here to listen. Consider, how can I understand and encourage?

Watch Film (10 minutes)
Propaganda – Identity

Discussion (45 minutes)
1. What did you connect with in Propaganda's sharing?
2. What "norms about manhood" do you think are influencing what you believe about yourself? How does that contrast with what God says about you?

Action (10 minutes)
In light of today's discussion, what is one step you can take in your life or in your relationships this week? Something specific. Something measurable. Something the group can pray for during the week.

Be mindful of the need for everyone to have an opportunity to talk. Take 2-3 minutes each. Take notes and pray for each other's action steps during the week. As always, keep everything confidential.

Closing Prayer
Ask for God's guidance and strength during the week ahead.

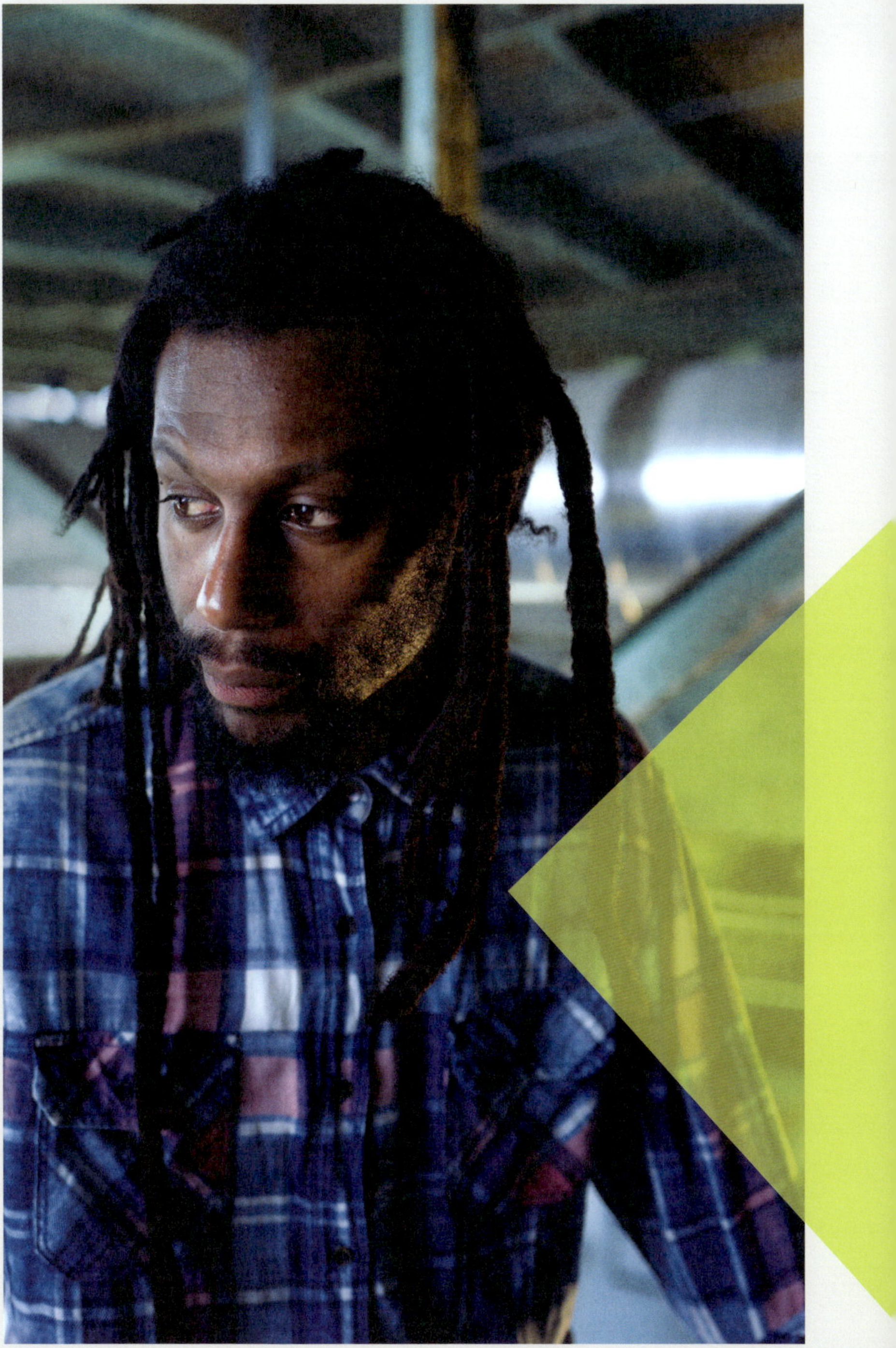

PERSONAL STUDY

EPISODE 9: PROPAGANDA - IDENTITY

Remember WHO YOU ARE man of God!

You ARE a chosen, forgiven, redeemed son of the Creator of the universe.

You ARE a commissioned minister of reconciliation.

You ARE co-heir with Christ to the Kingdom of Heaven.

And you ARE my brother.

In this film, Jason Petty, aka Propaganda, offers us a brilliant dissertation on identity, what forms it, what is our old identity, what is offered to us as a new identity and how we transition from one to the other.

First, let's think about this for a few moments. What is identity? It's your perception of who you are, why you are that way, and what you do to sustain that perception.

Life and the cultures we are born into offer us one identity and this is the first set of identities we take on. It's like a fish swimming in the water. The fish doesn't even think about water. It is just the environment they swim in. It is like the air we breathe. Air is what surrounds us. How often do you remind yourself to breathe? Not often, if at all. It's just the environment you were born into; you embraced it with your first breath and didn't give it another thought unless you were forced to.

This is how the identity we developed as children happened.

We just naturally, often automatically, took on points of view, beliefs and 'tribal affiliations' based on the primary influences in our life.

For example, if you like sports, what are your favorite sports teams? What are your political beliefs? What are your points of view on racial matters? There are hundreds of examples like this. Where you land on each of these matters has as much to do with what influences you had growing up as did your own independent thinking.

Many of the 'tribes' you are a part of now were automatically adopted, due to your place of origin, family of origin, geographical location of origin and the experiences you had. Often, we instinctually choose our preferences without much thought. And, then, somewhere along the way, you may start questioning the preferences you automatically took on.

Let's take a look at how Propaganda described this identity challenge. Consider his thoughts in light of how you may have built your own identity.

He noticed how he had formed his original identity growing up:

What he thought it meant to be a man...

"We were in this Latino neighborhood and what I knew from Latino men is, yo... men work, like that's what you do. They work long hours, hard hours. That's what men do.

So, if you ain't working, you ain't a real man."

REMEMBER WHO YOU ARE MAN OF GOD! YOU ARE A CHOSEN, FORGIVEN, REDEEMED SON OF THE CREATOR OF THE UNIVERSE. YOU ARE A COMMISSIONED MINISTER OF RECONCILIATION. YOU ARE CO-HEIR WITH CHRIST TO THE KINGDOM OF HEAVEN. AND **YOU ARE MY BROTHER.**

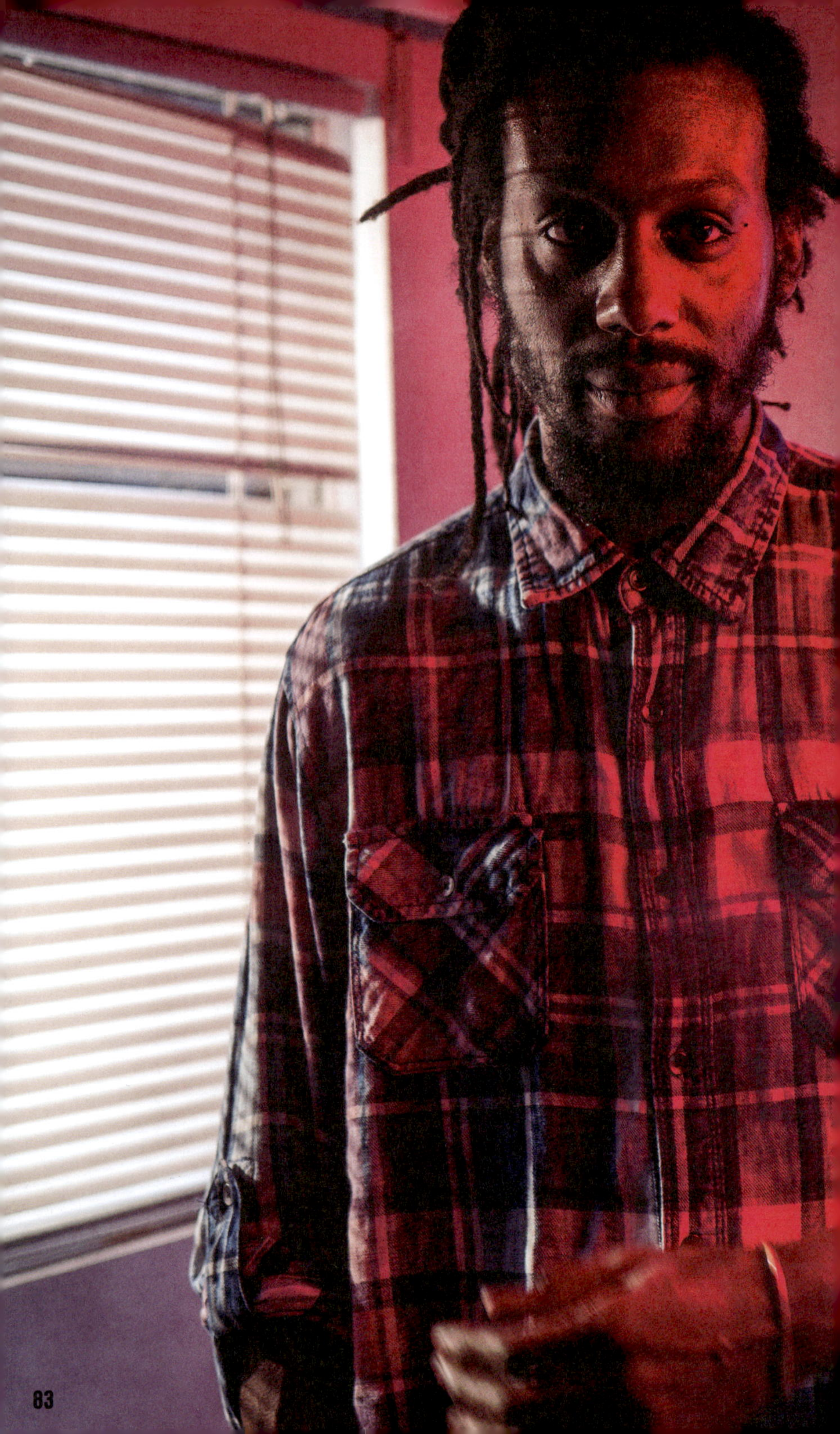

84

EPISODE 9

The allure and fallacy of the self-made man...

"I don't like the idea that somebody had to do something for me for me to get where I am. But it's such a dumb thing to not like because everything is like that, somebody did something for you."

You are what you do...

"I have a profession where our value is quantified by ticket sales and album sales. If you have friends that are killing it...doing better than you...oftentimes you feel like 'dang, like what am I doing? What am I doing wrong?' It starts becoming like super competition with buddies. And I think that's been such a hindrance in the sense that sometimes it sparks jealousy...like envy towards people that are your loved ones."

The ramifications of thinking you are what you do...

"But when I feel like I'm not as good as them or the world doesn't think I'm as good as them, I stop pursuing the fullness of who I am, and I'm just overwhelmed with who they are."

Building a new identity...

"So, what it means for my identity to be on purpose is that I don't have to see myself from a deficit model. A lot of times as dudes, we're like 'Yo, I worked hard. I struggled. You know I failed at this.' So, it's like you're starting from a deficit. And then mistakes happen. We look back like 'I shouldn't have done this or shouldn't have done that.' Again, it's a deficit. But if I say no, this is on purpose, I'm not starting from a deficit. I'm starting from purpose. Then moving forward is not reactionary or in regret. It's moving from design. If I can see my identity as a design like I'm black on purpose, and I'm from L.A. on purpose...I know what I've gone through was on purpose. Like God was painting something bigger. When I understand my life is that then.... Of course, it isn't to excuse mistakes or things that I had no control over. I don't see those as victim inducing. I see this as by design'

Expressing this new identity...

"I realize a lot of my definition of manhood was just misogyny and patriarchy, which is oppressive. And I've learned now as a married man and a grownup how quickly I can humble myself... Esteeming others higher than myself...leveraging power and privilege for others. For me now that is the mark of manhood. If I want to lead, then lead by service...lead through submission. Ultimately this is the call for all of us, but specifically as a dude, given the context of our culture, I want to lead by not trying to gain power but trying to lay it down. Now I feel like that's manhood."

Transitioning from the old identity to the new identity...

"Forgiveness was the father stooping down. And I think that that's such a challenge to our concept of manhood of you working to get yours. You get where you get because you grinded. That's the way I thought. What man meant was work. Nobody hands you anything. Everybody has the same 24 hours. I just need to make mine be 32. You know what I'm saying?

But forgiveness came out of the heart of the Father - not because of the actions of the receiver, which points us to the adoption part, which means you had no hand in this; but both of those things - they immediately humble and they level the playing field and they say 'You know this is the action. We are receivers, rather than givers.'"

We close with this final thought for you to consider from Propaganda...

"I think at the end of the day I would challenge men to challenge their norms. Question things that you figured were set in stone as far as our definitions of manhood, of strength, and beauty of leadership. I think when you're willing to really question and deconstruct, you can reconstruct into a better configuration. Sometimes winning is losing. Sometimes leading is to serve. It is to be humble and identity doesn't come solely from our experiences, but, from our Maker."

EPISODE 9
REFLECTION

PERSONAL STUDY QUESTIONS

1. Consider some of your identities you derived from the culture, location and family you were born into. How many aspects of your identity can you list as you consider this?

2. Consider your attitude towards others who are in 'tribes' that differ or oppose the group identities that you have adopted. Think specifics... your attitude towards those that have different points of view politically, religiously, opposing sports team fans, different ethnicities. What do you notice?

3. Reread this opening quote and consider how this is a better description of who you really are:

   > Remember WHO YOU ARE man of God!
   > You ARE a chosen, forgiven, redeemed son of the Creator of the universe.
   > You ARE a commissioned minister of reconciliation.
   > You ARE co-heir with Christ to the Kingdom of Heaven.
   > And you ARE my brother.

4. Have I addressed my Action step that I shared with my CORE Group? If not, what is keeping me from stepping out and addressing it? What's my next step?

JOURNALING:

Write your answers in your notebook. Also, journal about what comes to mind that can be applied to the specific areas in your life you are committed to taking new ground, as referenced in your vision you created in Session 1. What are you learning? What is happening? Where are you making progress? Where are you stuck? What's working? What's not working? What's wanted and needed? What's next?

SCRIPTURE REFLECTION:

We encourage you to consider this following scripture passage over the course of this week in a contemplative way. Read the passage four separate times. It works well if you read it on four separate days. Each time you read it, read it from a different perspective.

1. With the first reading, be alert for a phrase or word that stands out for you.

2. During the second reading, take a moment to reflect on what touches you, perhaps saying that particular verse out loud or writing it in your notebook.

3. After reading the passage a third time, respond with a prayer to God about what you have experienced and what the scripture might be calling you to.

4. Finally, rest in silence after a fourth reading, trusting that, *"it is God who works in you, both to will and to work for his good pleasure."*
Philippians 2:13 (ESV)

This process helps you to engage not only your mind, but your heart and soul in worshipful reflection on the scriptures. This can also give you fresh courage and trust to take new ground to where God is calling you forward.

This week's reflection scripture: **JEREMIAH 9:23-24 (ESV)**

Thus says the Lord:
"Let not the wise man boast in his wisdom,
let not the mighty man boast in his might,
let not the rich man boast in his riches,
but let him who boasts boast in this,
that he understands and knows me,
that I am the Lord who practices steadfast love,
justice, and righteousness in the earth.
For in these things I delight,
declares the Lord."

EPISODE 10

CLINT BRUCE
RELOAD

GROUP DISCUSSION GUIDE
90 MINUTES

Opening Prayer
Surrender time and heart to God's leading.

Check In (25 minutes)
Be mindful that you are not taking more time to talk than the others in the group.

1. How has your week gone? Family? Work?
2. What kind of progress or challenges did you have with your Action step?
3. How was your Personal Study and Scripture Reflection time this week? What is resonating? What is not working?

No judgment zone. Remember that we are here to listen. Consider, how can I understand and encourage?

Watch Film (10 minutes)
Clint Bruce - Reload

Discussion (45 minutes)
1. What part of Clint's story and sharing connected with you?
2. What high, hard ridgelines are you choosing to pursue?
3. What new ground have you taken during this CORE Series 1 journey?
4. What next steps would you like to pursue with your CORE group?

Action (10 minutes)
In light of today's discussion, what is one step you can take in your life or in your relationships this week? Something specific. Something measurable. Something the group can pray for during the week.

Be mindful of the need for everyone to have an opportunity to talk. Take 2-3 minutes each. Take notes and pray for each other's action steps during the week. As always, keep everything confidential.

Closing Prayer
Ask for God's guidance and strength during the week ahead and if and how you are to continue as a group.

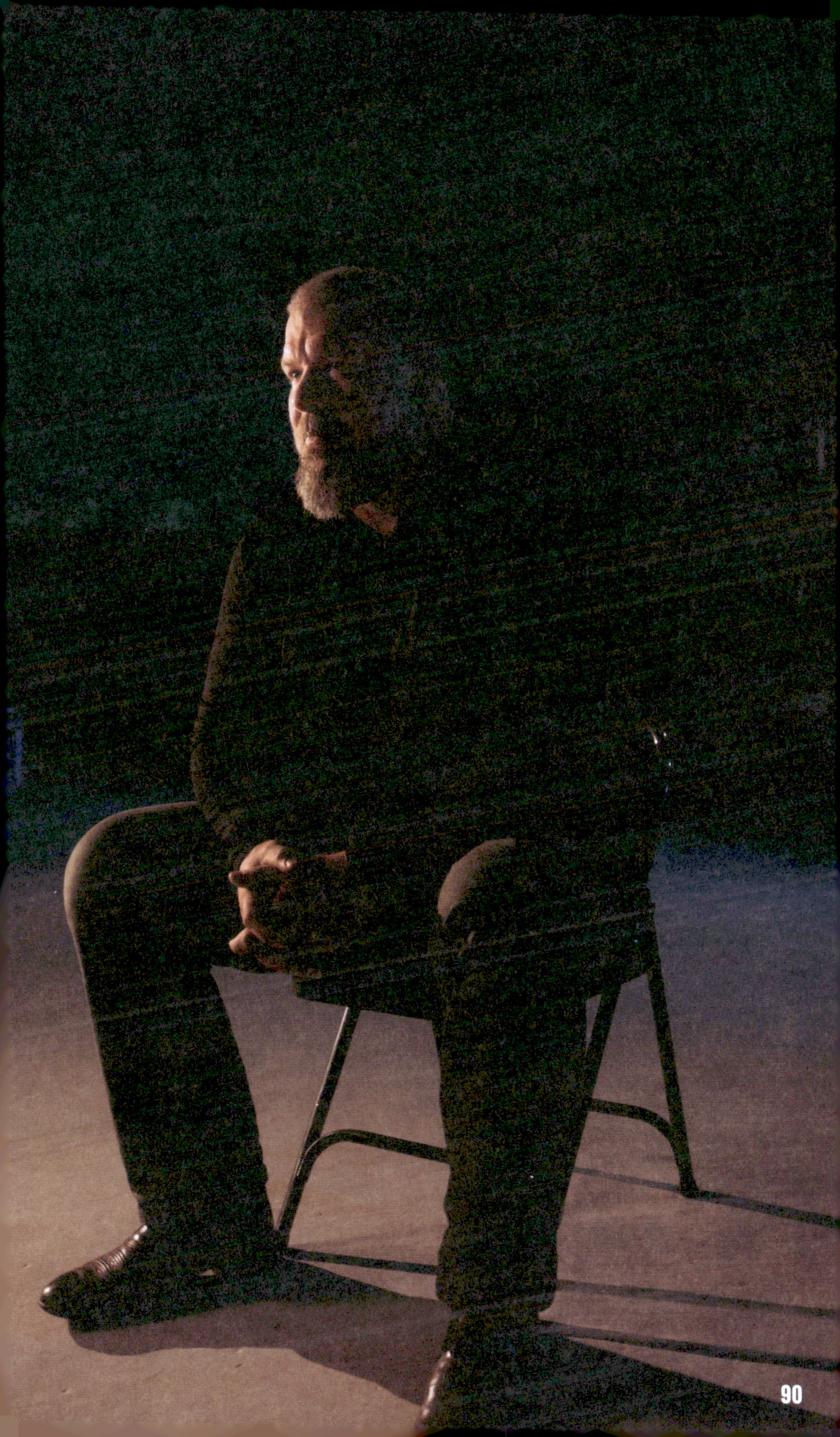

PERSONAL STUDY

EPISODE 10: CLINT BRUCE - RELOAD

"Use your time for what matters." This is the final thing Clint Bruce says in his film.

So, let's recall what you said matters to you in the very first session of this CORE journey. In that first session, we asked you to consider this:

- Where can you use a breakthrough? Consider your key relationships, your personal life, your family life, your work life, and your community life.
- What fears do you have of even hoping for this kind of change?

If you kept a notebook, re-read it. If not, try and recall where you were when you started this. What are you seeing? What themes and trends are happening? What are you learning? What new Action steps are you taking? What attitudes are shifting?

As we discuss Clint Bruce's story, consider what he is saying within the areas of your life you have chosen to work on.

Ask yourself, "How can I actually apply this in my life?" Moving these insights into actual practices is the key. The goal moving forward is not to simply grow in more knowledge of what could be or should be. The aim is not to listen, be challenged, and then tuck the information away somewhere safe. Instead, actual and practical life-change is the objective of this session, these 10 weeks, and ultimately the objective of life. Like all that have gone before you, it means risk, failure, learning and breakthrough.

Clint refers to something called a "ridgeline". A ridgeline is the highest edge of a mountain. It is the hardest place to get to, but it is also the place that provides the best protection and perspective. It's the place to celebrate the letting go of old ground and planning what it will take to advance into new ground.

To get to the ridgeline, you have to make tremendous sacrifice and you must equip yourself with the tools and the friendships around you to make the climb. Through the rigorous process of traversing each ridgeline in your life, you will become more and more "elite".

Clint says that for him, "Elite is just a little more than what you thought you could do before you get to excellent. And, living this way is a reflection of being a steward of your time."

Think of this in terms of your own purpose and calling in life. God has given you a new identity. My identity is not what others think about me, it's not what I think about me, it's what God believes about me. Out of this foundation he has an overarching purpose for all of us... to create flourishing in life everywhere we go... in every relationship, in every circumstance, in every exchange, in all things large and small.

God has given you a specific calling that is unique to you. It may take years and years for you to fully discover this, and that's okay. You go with what you are passionate about now, using the gifts you see God has given you, while staying open to God's leading as you move forward.

Think about your calling and purpose

I FAILED MY WAY TO SUCCESS.

Thomas Edison

EPISODE 10

in light of what Clint said about stewardship. How we pursue our calling and purpose is a reflection of how we steward our time.

How much time do we have left? Not one of us knows the answer to this question. Pursuing elite is a reflection of urgency, because our days on this earth have an expiration date.

Clint draws the distinction between relaxing and reloading - the practice of how we choose to rest. Rest is a largely ignored spiritual discipline in our culture. The biblical concept of rest is much more than the absence of work. A day off. A vacation. The idea of observing 'Sabbath', where we dedicate a day to unplug from responsibilities and spend that time with family and the community of faith is certainly rest. Practicing times of silence and solitude is rest.

When all that you do comes out of gratitude for Christ's love, it produces a supernatural rest unlike anything you could generate by yourself. This kind of rest allows you to begin the hard work of shedding the weight of needing to prove yourself and your worth.

So then, there remains a Sabbath rest for the people of God, for whoever has entered God's rest has also rested from his works as God did from his. **Hebrews 4:9-10 (ESV)**

Some may perceive rest as a lack of motivation or laziness. Maybe you've found yourself thinking, "I have too much to do. I have no time for this!" Perhaps you have heard yourself say, "well, you don't understand my schedule and responsibilities. I don't have time to rest." The fact is that rest is also action. It is a receptive, restorative action, rather than an assertive action. Our culture is all about go, go, go. **We have lost the critical importance of rest as a preparation for effective action.**

Rest, from a scriptural point of view, is a reloading with the understanding of Christ's finished work. Because of his death on our behalf, we are already his beloved children.
(Ephesians 1:5-7)

It is out of this awareness that we can be infused with motivation to enter into His purpose and vision for our life. It is a chance to reconnect to God and notice how we can be more fully present when we are in action.

Contemplative spiritual practices prepare us to reload and take action in a meaningful way. Contemplation on the truth and faith in action are joined at the hip. They are inseparable.

Reloading is getting grounded into what matters, in order to be prepared for what's next. Relaxing is different, as Clint describes it. Relaxing is seeking out rest for rest's sake, pleasure for pleasure's sake. It's self-focused. It's the end in and of itself. There is no ridgeline or specific vision attached to it.

Clint says, "David is such a great lesson in passion and authenticity and asking for grace."

"I don't know that you really know how to pray unless you read Psalms, because when you read Psalms you're able to pray in a much more honest and raw way. David is perhaps the most encouraging Biblical figure that we go back to because of his fallibility and how often he was a train wreck."

"Sometimes, many of us wonder if we're worth it. We often do these reckless things because we're just not sure if our actions or inactions have any real impact on anybody."

"DAVID WAS EVERY CRASH AND BURN THAT WE'VE SEEN IN THE LAST FIFTY YEARS IN SPORTS AND POLITICS AND BUSINESS ALL ROLLED UP IN ONE GUY. WHAT I THINK SAVED DAVID ALL THE TIME IS THAT AWARENESS OF WHO HE WAS AND THAT HE HAD BEEN PICKED AND WHY HE WAS THERE."

We have this transcendent, amazing God who helps you know that you are worth it because he created you. Consistent times of reloading are moments that God reminds you of your worth. If all you do is go and go and go without stopping to reload, then you'll start believing that your worth is tied to your successes, or lack thereof.

I can't seem to make my sales quota.

I must be a horrible worker. I'm such a failure.

I can't seem to find a job I actually enjoy, maybe I'll never find that. I probably don't deserve it anyway. Maybe that's an unrealistic expectation.

Money is so tight each month. Why can't I provide in a way that takes all the stress off of my family. What is wrong with me? I probably won't ever get this figured out."

Do any of these statements sound familiar?

You are NOT taking ridgelines to prove your worth. You take ridgelines because your worth has already been secured in Jesus. Now, you don't have to fear taking new ridgelines. You are free to climb. Clint continues,

"And I think that was David's great gift. It was the ability to just believe what God said when God talked about David. Every time he relaxed instead of reloading he messed up with the absence of that ridgeline. The absence of that high hard thing that we're going to is where I made my most tremendous mistakes. This happens when I haven't clarified or remembered the high hard ridgelines I'm going to, and also when I forget tying it all into the accountability of others."

Having a great marriage is a high hard ridgeline. Raising kids to be healthy, responsible adults is a high, hard ridgeline. Creating flourishing in your work life is a high, hard ridgeline. Pursuing your purpose and calling without being distracted from it is a high, hard ridgeline. All of these require the same disciplines that Clint Bruce references in the context of his Navy Seal days.

He says, "life is very much the series of picking a high ridgeline in it and then try, fail, fix, try again, and you do that over and over again. It's really hard to do that when you're wandering but if you're patrolling and if you're moving towards a target...if you're moving toward something that you decide is important to you and important to what you stand for...then that's just the process.

EPISODE 10

What I've learned is you have to get to create those ridgelines."

"Those are all opportunities to put what you believe to work and to try and to fail and to fix and try again. It truly is all about whether you're willing to suffer. I don't like suffering for suffering's sake. There's got to be a reason that helps you pull through that resistance. And for me suffering has always been the barometer for someone's ability to do great things. Can they suffer, or will they suffer?

When you suffer because life is not showing up the way you prefer or the way you intended, what are you going to do? Usually, we escape the suffering by trying to numb and distance ourselves, instead of reloading. Reloading embraces rest and reflection as we consider what isn't working, what's needed, what's next to go again.

This isn't just for Navy Seals in battle. This is for every single person. Regardless of your history, your personality, your temperament, your confidence, your IQ or your savvy. Trying, failing, fixing and, trying again is the charge for each and every one of us. It's the charge for you.

This is how you make a dent in the world with your purpose and calling.

In fact, you could say this is at the very CORE of what we are about.

Thank you for joining in with us on this CORE journey! Our deepest desire is for you to continue with a CORE group and lean into them as a resource and opportunity to serve and grow together. We have many more learning and action opportunities that you can utilize, and we hope they are an encouragement to you as you engage them.

Our desire is for you to be a powerful force for good...

- In your family
- In your church
- In your workplace
- In your city
- In the world

The greatest guidebook ever developed to do this is your Bible. The greatest and highest honor is to be called by God - not something we even remotely deserved but have been gifted by God's grace.

Now, let's do something about it!

Use your time, for what matters.

"My prayer is that when I die, all of hell rejoices that I am out of the fight." –Unknown

EPISODE 10
REFLECTION

PERSONAL STUDY QUESTIONS

1. What high, hard ridgelines are you pursuing in your life?
2. What new ground have you taken in the last ten weeks?
3. What is wanted and needed, moving forward?
4. What's next for your CORE group? Visit us on our web site, **coreunites.com**, to get the latest resources to support your group in your journey together.
5. You can also follow us on social media **@coreunites**.

JOURNALING:

Write your answers in your notebook. Also, journal about what comes to mind that can be applied to the specific areas in your life you are committed to taking new ground, as referenced in your vision you created in Session 1. What are you learning? What is happening? Where are you making progress? Where are you stuck? What's working? What's not working? What's wanted and needed? What's next?